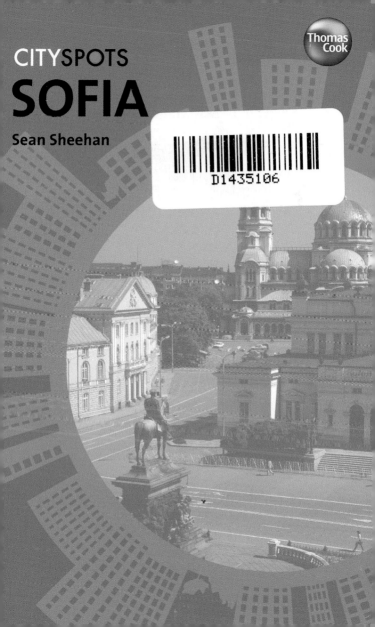

Thomas Cook

CITYSPOTS
SOFIA

Sean Sheehan

D1435106

Written by Sean Sheehan
Updated by Poli Mihaylova

Published by Thomas Cook Publishing
A division of Thomas Cook Tour Operations Limited
Company registration No: 1450464 England
The Thomas Cook Business Park, 9 Coningsby Road
Peterborough PE3 8SB, United Kingdom
Email: books@thomascook.com, Tel: +44 (0)1733 416477
www.thomascookpublishing.com

Produced by The Content Works Ltd
Aston Court, Kingsmead Business Park, Frederick Place
High Wycombe, Bucks HP11 1LA
www.thecontentworks.com

Series design based on an original concept by Studio 183 Limited

ISBN: 978-1-84157-967-2

First edition © 2006 Thomas Cook Publishing
This second edition © 2008 Thomas Cook Publishing
Text © Thomas Cook Publishing
Maps © Thomas Cook Publishing/PCGraphics (UK) Limited
Transport map © Communicarta Limited

Series Editor: Kelly Anne Pipes
Production/DTP: Steven Collins

Printed and bound in Spain by GraphyCems

Cover photography (Sveta Sofia church) © Dominic Whiting/Alamy

CONTENTS

SYMBOLS KEY

The following symbols are used throughout this book:

ⓐ address ⓣ telephone ⓕ fax ⓦ website address ⓔ email
ⓛ opening times ⓝ public transport connections ⓘ important

The following symbols are used on the maps:

𝒊	information office	▦	points of interest
✈	airport	O	city
✚	hospital	O	large town
⬟	police station	○	small town
▥	bus station	=	motorway
▤	railway station	—	main road
✝	cathedral	—	minor road
❶	numbers denote featured	—	railway
	cafés & restaurants		

Hotels and restaurants are graded by approximate price as follows:
£ budget price ££ mid-range price £££ expensive

The following abbreviations are used for addresses:
blvd.   boulevard
sq.   square

◗ *View of Sofia from Mount Vitosha*

Introduction

One of Europe's youngest capital cities – only established as such in 1879 – has all the attractiveness of precocious youth: unsophisticated, vigorously alive, relishing an undiluted urge for fun and late nights. Remarkably inexpensive bars, cafés, restaurants, pubs and piano bars are everywhere and closing times for all such places are commonly two in the morning, seven days a week. Less than a decade ago, no one could have imagined that staid and stodgy Sofia would morph into an epicurean outpost in the bleak Balkans. The metamorphosis is ongoing, and when you settle into a café-restaurant-bar – Sofia's secular trinity – you too become part of the process and start to soak up the unique character of this most surprising of European capitals.

Sofia is compact, and the hotels, restaurants and bars that will compete for your time are nearly all located within a tidily arranged city centre that is minutes from the airport. The city has a distinct European flavour with its broad boulevards and countless number of open-air watering holes, but there are intriguing reminders of its more Eastern heritage in the form of Byzantine- and Russian-inspired churches. The most immediate, and daily, reminder that that you are deep inside Eastern Europe comes when you grapple with street and place names that use the Cyrillic alphabet. It is part of the fun of being somewhere different, and you cannot get seriously lost because the city centre is too small. Trams and cheap taxis will take you anywhere that is not within walking distance.

What may at first seem a deficit of conventional attractions turns out to be a refreshing lack of manufactured tourism. There are museums and galleries to visit, but not so many as to exhaust yourself tramping from one must-see sight to another. Two or three days will easily cover the ground, and if your stay is any longer then it is time to take an excursion. There are two neighbouring towns with very contrasting characters, and the ski slopes at Mount Vitosha are a convenient six-minute bus ride away from one of the city's bus terminals.

⬤ *The city centre is filled with both historical buildings and green spaces*

When to go

As long as you have no objections to the snow and freezing temperatures of the winter months (when you'll always be able to find countless wonderful ways of keeping warm), Sofia is a great place to visit at any time.

SEASONS & CLIMATE

Sofia's climate is continental, and while the summers are hot and sunny, the winter months can be very cold. January is the coldest, with the mercury dipping below zero at night, and the months either side are not noticeably different. This is certainly not a problem if skiing is on your agenda and you are above 800 m (2,625 ft) to enjoy blue skies and crisp snow. On sunny days, the daytime temperature can be 20°C (68°F) in the sun, though well below zero at night. Come March, temperatures start rising to around 5°C (41°F) and continue to rise steadily each month for the next three months. April to June is a lovely time to be in Sofia, with al fresco eating and drinking being the order of the day; the weather is ideal for excursions into the countryside and airfares have not peaked. The public parks become attractions in their own right and are ideal for long picnics. In June the temperature is 19°C (66°F) and stays in the mid-20s°C (70s°F) throughout July and August, the hottest months of the year, until dropping back to June's average in September. Temperatures then plummet steadily each month, and by the end of November the first snow has fallen above 1,000 m (3,281 ft). December brings the freezing cold once more, and throughout the winter months Sofia is usually covered by a grey and heavy smog, making this period the least attractive time to make a visit (especially when fog causes flight delays at the airport).

ANNUAL EVENTS

March

International Women's Day (8 Mar) A day when the guys show the gals just how much they appreciate them.

Sofia International Film Festival The first half of March brings this festival, now well over ten years old and still going strong.
① (02) 916 6029 **Ⓦ** www.cinema.bg/sff

April

Easter Sunday (19 Apr 2009; 4 Apr 2010) Easter according to the Eastern Orthodox calendar falls later than in the Catholic or Protestant churches. Midnight Mass is held, special food prepared and a festival of classical and choir music takes place in the city's churches.

April & May

Drama Festival Stretching over late April and early May, a drama festival takes place in venues across the city.

MARCH & MARTENITSAS

At the start of March it is time to present friends and relatives with martenitsas – entwined red-and-white woollen threads – to bring them happiness and health. Sold everywhere, they are worn on clothing or tied around the wrist until, so the tradition goes, the first stork is seen. Sofia is not exactly overcrowded with storks, but by the end of the month people follow the custom of tying their martenitsas on to a fruit tree in a park or garden.

May & June
Festival of Classical Music and Ballet The main venue for this culture fest is, appropriately, the National Palace of Culture (NDK, see page 94). Tickets can be bought in advance at the **NDK ticket office** (📞 (02) 916 6369 🌐 www.ndk.bg).

August
Regional Folk Music Festival Over the weekend closest to 15 August, a regional folk music festival takes place in the small town of Koprivshtitsa (see page 136).

🔺 *Fountains at the National Palace of Culture*

November
International Jazz Festival This takes place in Sofia in the second week of the month.

December–April
The skiing season Come December, there is usually enough snow on Mount Vitosha (see page 116) to kick-start the skiing season. Most years, it effectively ends at the end of March, though it can linger into April.

PUBLIC HOLIDAYS
New Year's Day 1 Jan
Liberation Day 3 Mar
Easter Sunday 19 Apr 2009; 4 Apr 2010
Labour Day 1 May
Bulgarian Army Day 6 May
Day of the Cyrillic Alphabet and
   Bulgarian Education and Culture 24 May
Unification Day 6 Sept
Independence Day 22 Sept
Christmas Eve 24 Dec
Christmas Day 25 & 26 Dec

Banks, post offices, government offices and many shops and businesses are closed on public holidays, but restaurants and bars are not affected and public transport runs according to the usual schedules.

Architectural affluence

The gift of beauty can often lead to an eventful life, and the greatest legacy of Sofia's undeniably tumultuous history is the huge number of fabulous buildings that are dotted all around the city. Its architectural spectrum encompasses an unusual mix that includes Byzantine-inspired churches and Soviet-influenced socialist art. The colonnaded former headquarters of the Central Committee of the Communist Party (see page 66) still asserts itself, in a butch architectural fashion at least, while only a short walk away stands a magnificent contrast in the neo-Byzantine form of the Alexander Nevsky Memorial Church (see page 80).

Equally impressive is the essentially art nouveau interior (though there are hints of Vienna Secession and, intriguingly, Moorish Revival) of the city's synagogue (see page 69), whose voluptuousness bears eloquent testimony to Bulgaria's tremendous act of protecting its Jewish population in World War II. The Soviet Army Monument (see page 106) is also tremendously affective. Although it is reviled by some Bulgarians because of the odious associations with the Soviet era that followed the end of World War II, it is a superb example of monumental sculpture and the best piece of public art in the city. Friezes around the base, depicting scenes of men and women fighting, are remarkably dynamic and convey a dramatic sense of movement. Confronting a brave new future, 34 m (111 1/2 ft) above these scenes, a Red Army soldier stands in solidarity with a worker and a peasant woman with her child. The icing on the architectural cake takes high-spirited form in the neo-wacky Russian Church (see page 83), built in 1913 for an ultra devout diplomat from the soon-to-be-toppled Tsarist empire.

Trips out of the city will only add to your architectural pleasure. Koprivshtitsa, a small town 75 km (46 1/2 miles) to the east of Sofia, is noted for its traditional Bulgarian architecture, of which you'll find an enchanting example in Todor Kableshkov House (see page 138). The curvy lines of each side of its façade are a characteristic feature of the vernacular architecture. A cracking example of Bulgarian religious construction is found in the Rila Monastery (see page 130), whose fortress-like appearance and out-of-town location both attest to the beleaguered state of Christianity when Bulgaria was part of the Ottoman Empire (see page 14).

🔺 *Sofia Synagogue*

History

Bulgaria was known as Thrace to the ancient Greeks and to the Romans who conquered the land and made possible its incorporation into the Byzantine Empire that was ruled from Constantinople (Istanbul). Slavs migrated into the region and mixed with the nomadic Bulgars, laying the basis for a Bulgarian kingdom that succumbed to the power of the Ottoman Empire in the late 14th century. It was half a millennium later, with the help of Russian support for Slav independence, that a war of liberation against Turkish rule finally proved effective and the Treaty of San Stefano in 1878 recognised a liberated Bulgaria.

Bulgaria fell to the Nazis in World War II but, heroically and almost uniquely, Bulgarian public opinion resisted Nazi demands and the willingness of their Nazi puppet government for the country's Jews to be transported to the death camps. After the war, the Bulgarian Communist Party emerged to take political control and the country became part of the Soviet bloc under the dictatorial rule of Todor Zhivkov. The Cold War period gave Bulgarians guaranteed work and free medical care, but the country's image suffered in the West. The secret police were blamed for the murder of dissident writer Georgi Markov, murdered on London's Waterloo Bridge in 1978 after being stabbed by a poison-tipped umbrella. Human rights campaigners drew attention to the persecution of racial minorities in Bulgaria itself. Sofia, none too surprisingly, was not a favourite holiday destination for Westerners.

The winds of change fanned by Gorbachev in Moscow swept into Bulgaria, and by the late 1980s economic and political life was beginning to change radically. As elsewhere in Eastern Europe, events moved swiftly and dramatically. On 10 November 1989, the day after the Berlin Wall came down, a power struggle and ideological split within the ruling party led to the removal of the old order – Zhivkov exited stage left – and the promise of free elections and a multiparty system. A new government emerged after elections in 1991, and the old system was dismantled. However, the unleashing of an untamed capitalism led to widespread inequities as the gap between rich and poor widened obscenely and polarised the country. By 1996, hyper-inflation was reaching nearly 600 per cent and crippling the country. Street protests and strikes in 1997 led to a new caretaker government under the popular mayor of Sofia, and relative stability emerged from the chaos. The social divisions, nonetheless, remained, and these help to explain the strange events of 2001. Simeon Saxe-Coburg Gotha, Tsar in exile since he was expelled by the Communists after World War II, returned to the country only two months before parliamentary elections. He formed a new party, promising to stamp out corruption, and he won with a landslide victory. In 2004, Bulgaria joined NATO, and on 1 January 2007 Bulgaria became a full member of the EU. Now established on that economic launchpad, Bulgaria is ready for lift-off. Watch this space.

Detail from the façade of the National Theatre

Lifestyle

The lifestyle encountered in the city centre is recognisably that of continental Europe, characterised by a predominantly young population, with familiar brand names in the shop windows and advertisements for mobile phones. The pace of life may be slower than you are used to, and there is a pleasantly relaxed start to working days; weekends, by comparison, seem comatose. Young people learn English as their second language (their parents learned Russian), and their general level of education is high. While you cannot assume that English is generally understood, young people working in hotels and restaurants understand your needs and are usually more than willing to help.

While the lifestyle is Western European – and with a hedonistic vengeance when it comes to pavement cafés and bars – one aspect of Sofia that is decidedly Eastern is the alphabet. Sofia uses the Cyrillic alphabet, as used in Russia, Ukraine and Serbia. What will confuse you is that although some of the 30 letters look the same as Latin ones, they are pronounced very differently. A typical example is the word 'ресторант' – which you will be tempted to read as 'pectopaht' – which means 'restaurant'. The briefest look at the Cyrillic alphabet (see page 56) will pay dividends when it comes to deciphering street and place names.

There is another lifestyle in Sofia, the one lived by an older generation that has had to cope with the momentous changes associated with the transition from a state-governed economy to a capitalist one, and the shift from a Balkan to a more Western European culture. It can be observed and appreciated in the Women's Market in the centre of the city (see page 70) – this is where ordinary people come to buy their clothes, food and other provisions – and here you will see the older lifestyle still ticking away. Shoppers in the market know how to judge the freshness of the fruits and vegetables on the stalls and they know the value of every cent. To enjoy and understand Sofia means acknowledging both these lifestyles.

◐ *Graffiti comes in Cyrillic, too*

Culture

The decades of subjugation under authoritarian, pro-Soviet governments fostered aspects of cultural development that were seen as intrinsically worthwhile but not threatening to the status quo. The legacy of this is that Sofia is home to a wealth of musical and theatrical establishments and, although the visitor that doesn't understand Bulgarian is handicapped when it comes to drama, there are wonderful opportunities to enjoy opera, ballet and classical music. Spring, when musical festivities get underway, is the best time to enjoy these art forms although whatever the time of year, ticket prices are always wonderfully affordable. The Sofia Philharmonic Orchestra performs regularly, and the National Opera has a repertoire of internationally recognised operas and ballets. Musicals and operettas from around the world are performed, from *Die Fledermaus* to *Evita*, and although performances are in Bulgarian they can still be hugely enjoyable.

Bulgaria's traditional culture is well represented at the National Ethnographic Museum (see page 71), housed in the former Royal Palace, which also plays host to international exhibitions. The most important collections, principally Thracian gold and silver treasures, have their home at the National History Museum (see page 109), situated at Boyana, to the south of the city, although the Thracian collection is often out of the country. In the same neighbourhood stands Boyana Church (see page 106), famous for its fragile frescoes from the medieval age. Back in the city centre, the National Archaeological Museum (see page 70) has a number of interesting finds that date back to the time of ancient Greece and Rome.

● *Check out the sculptures at the Puta Gallery*

The National Art Gallery is in Sofia (see page 71), but many visitors find more engaging art work in the National Gallery of Foreign Art (see page 84) and in smaller establishments like the Sofia City Art Gallery (see page 73), where changing exhibitions are likely to offer something interesting. New artistic endeavours, especially in painting and sculpture, are also to be found in a number of small, private galleries dotted around the city. In these galleries, original art work is for sale and often at very agreeable prices. This art scene is a shifting and ongoing one, but the relevant sections of the free city guides will highlight new galleries that have opened up and attracted attention.

▶ *Clashing architectural styles in Nezavisimost Square*

Shopping

Shopping is an art form of its own in Sofia, and to find something interesting you often need to hunt down individual shops and stores. Fashionable Vitosha Boulevard, in the heart of the city, is a concentrated shopping area, particularly for clothing. It is pedestrianised, and so ideal for window shopping; a drawback for some, however, is that the outlets tend to focus on familiar Western brands. The same is true of Tzum (see page 74). Now a modern shopping mall, but once the state-owned department store, it's always justified its name, 'central universal shop' (the Bulgarian for which renders the abbreviated form 'Tzum'). Two other shopping centres are very popular. City Center Sofia (see page 110) and **Mall of Sofia** (ⓐ Alexander Stamboliiski Blvd. 101 ⓣ (02) 929 3377 ⓦ www.mallofsofia.com) both have a great number of shops selling international brand-names, many cafés and restaurants, as well as modern multiplex cinemas.

More rewarding in many ways is the narrow Tsar Shishman Street, easy to find because it starts next to the Radisson SAS Grand Hotel (see page 41), and home to a number of small, proprietor-run shops. As with Vitosha Boulevard, the emphasis is on clothing but the boutiques are more individual and each place has its own tiny but unique collection. Across Sofia as a whole, boutiques for women easily outnumber their counterparts for men.

Pedestrianised Pirotska Street, where there are more boutiques, leads to the southern end of Zhenski Pazar, the Women's Market (see page 70). Crammed with stalls and shoppers, this is the place to buy a jar of fresh honey or stock up on your supply of vegetable

---

◗ Matryoshka *dolls for sale at the Alexander Nevsky Square market*

seeds. The best market of all, in terms of finding something to bring home, is in front of the Alexander Nevsky Memorial Church (see page 80).

For original Bulgarian art, the area worth exploring is around Parizh Street, close to the Alexander Nevsky Memorial Church and the National Opera (see page 84). Here you will find a number of small galleries promoting the work of a new generation of young artists who work in a variety of styles from the expressive to the pictorial. An export licence may be required for some purchases, but the shops can arrange this.

An increasing number of shops will accept credit cards, and the relevant logos will be visible by the entrance or the till, but you may come across places that do not and the only option is to pay cash.

● *Pedestrianised Vitosha Boulevard is the main shopping street in Sofia*

USEFUL SHOPPING PHRASES

What time do the shops open/close?
В колко часа отварят/затварят магазините?
V kolko chasa otvaryat/zatvaryat magazinite?

How much is this?
Колко струва това?
Kolko struva tova?

Can I try this on?
Може ли да го пробвам?
Mozhe li da go probvam?

My size is...
Моят размер е...
Moyat razmer eh...

I'll take this one, thank you
Ще взема този, благодаря
Shte vzema tozi, blagodarya

This is too large/too small/too expensive.
Do you have any others?
Това е много голямо/малко/скъпо. Имате ли други?
Tova eh mnogo golyamo/malko/skapo. Imateh li drugi?

Eating & drinking

It is never a problem finding somewhere to eat and drink in Sofia. Prices are remarkably low, and often the more traditional Bulgarian dishes are preferable to Western European favourites. Standards of service vary, and you can be very pleased one day only to return another time and experience poor service, delays and confusion; this is all part of the city's learning curve rather than culpable lapses in standards. As a general rule, be as explicit as possible and try to check that your order has been understood.

Just about every menu begins with a list of various salads and among these there is nearly always a *shopska*. Almost a national dish, a *shopska* is made with chopped tomatoes, cucumber, peppers and onion, topped with white cheese. The *ovcharska* salad is similar but comes with grated egg and mushrooms. Equally popular is *snezhanka*, chopped cucumber with garlic mixed together in yogurt. For vegetarians, one of the salads followed by a hot starter makes

PRICE CATEGORIES

The following approximate price bands are based on the average cost of a three-course meal for one person, excluding drinks, and are indicated by these symbols:

£ up to €7.50 ££ €7.50–15 £££ over €15

In even the most expensive restaurants, you would seriously need to push the boat out in order to pay more than €25 for a three-course meal.

● *Vitosha Boulevard from the Upstairs bar*

a suitable meal at lunchtime. Hot starters feature stuffed or roasted peppers and tend to avoid meat.

Soups feature on most menus and the ones most likely to appear include *bob chorba* (bean soup) and *shkembe chorba* (tripe soup). Vegetarians should look for *tarator* in the warm months – a refreshing, cold soup composed of yogurt and cucumber with garlic.

Main courses are usually based around meat, with chicken, pork and veal being the firm favourites, and grilled meats are very common. Expect to find *kyufteta* (meat balls), *parzhola* (chops) and *kebapcheta* (elongated meat balls). The choice of fish can be disappointing and usually comes down to *pasturva* (trout) and the seasonal offering from the Black Sea. Desserts are a real let-down, and finding yourself tempted by wicked chocolate concoctions is, sadly, all too rare an experience. However, ice cream is popular and of good quality.

Sofia has no shortage of places to drink, and even the humblest café or kiosk tends to stock a range of soft drinks, beers and spirits. Cappuccinos feature on many menus, but prepare to be disappointed when a powdery substance stirred limply into life with a modicum of froth arrives on your table. Regular coffee, often just called American, may be too strong or just plain dire. Tea is widely available but unless you specifically ask for *cheren chay* (black tea), you will receive a herbal teabag without milk.

The most popular spirit is *rakiya*, a brandy made mainly from plums and grapes. It is traditionally drunk with a salad as an aperitif and, with 40 per cent alcohol, packs a punch. *Rakiya* and other spirits are listed in menus as 'small' (50 g/1 3/4 oz and roughly equivalent to a British double) or 'large' (100 g/3 1/2 oz), and there is often a variety of brands and prices to choose from. Burgas 63 is a good brand of *rakiya* for both plum and grape varieties; Troyanska

USEFUL DINING PHRASES

I would like a table for ... people
Бих искал маса за ... души
Bih iskal masa za ... dushi

Waiter/waitress!
Келнер!
Kelner!

Could I have it well-cooked/medium/rare please?
Може ли да го приготвите добре/опечено/
средно опечено, моля?
Mozhe li da go prigotvite dobre/sredno/leko opecheno, molya?

I am a vegetarian. Does this contain meat?
Аз съм вегетарианец. Има ли месо тук?
Az sum vegetarianets. Ima li mesoh tuk?

Where is the toilet (restroom) please?
Къде е тоалетната, моля?
Kadeh eh toaletnata, molya?

I would like a cup of/two cups of/another coffee/tea
Искам чаша/две чаши/още една чаша кафе/чай
Iskam chasha/dve chashi/oshteh edna chasha kafeh/chai

May I have the bill, please?
Сметката, моля?
Smetkata, molya?

is one of the better plum brandies; and Peshterska muskatova is a good grape equivalent.

Bulgarian wines are not as bad as you might suspect, and familiar grapes like Merlot and Cabernet Sauvignon have been grown with notable success. Mavrud is a Bulgarian grape variety, and the wine is worth tasting if you like a beefsteak quality to your wine. Bulgarian beers are palatable but not habit-forming, and imported Danish, German and Czech beers are commonly available.

Most restaurants are open seven days a week from between 10.00 and 11.00 onwards, closing around 23.00 or later. A service charge is not usually added to the bill and a tip of ten per cent is normally expected. By law, all restaurants should have a designated non-smoking area, but this is invariably a nominal affair. Wine lists in restaurants tend to be based around Bulgarian wines, and only the more expensive places will feature international selections. Half bottles are rarely listed on menus, but most places have no problem serving their wines by the glass. Meal prices are remarkably low by Western European standards and this goes some way in compensating for inconsistencies in standards and service.

◀ *Sofia bean casserole is a typical Bulgarian meal*

Entertainment & nightlife

Sofia's entertainment scene is broadly night-based and you will be surprised at the sheer number of bars, nightclubs and pubs that light up after dark and remain busy until the early hours of the morning. There is the usual gamut of so-called Irish pubs and Buddha bars, but it is more interesting to seek out some of the small bars and clubs where young Bulgarians party away the night, and up-and-coming musicians try to make a breakthrough. (Please note that some of the establishments listed in this guide have no phone number in their practical details – that's because sometimes the only number for some venues is the mobile number of its proprietor!) Piano bars are popular in a low-key kind of way, and provide a musical alternative to loud doses of pop rock. There are no cover charges in the clubs, and there is usually a drinks list in English. The Bulgarian for 'cheers' is *nazdrave*, meaning 'good health' and, if you find yourself in a group toasting, etiquette demands that you clink your glass with each and every person in the group looking them in the eye at the point of clinking (otherwise it will be taken as impoliteness).

Bulgarian folk music usually takes the form of *chalga* – shaking up the body and waggling limbs to a hybrid ethno-pop sound. In visitor-oriented restaurants staff are decked out in Arabian Nights costumes, but the shows are not as tacky as you might fear. Where some caution should be exercised is with the more lurid-looking nightclubs that obviously aim to draw in an adult male audience; it is not unknown for a hapless punter to be landed with a heavy bill and given no option but to pay up. The casinos that announce their presence in neon are best only patronised by the experienced.

There are wonderful opportunities to enjoy Sofia's interest in ballet and classical music – one of the legacies of the Soviet era –

and the free listings magazines carry details of current shows and performances. The main venue is the National Palace of Culture (often referred to as the NDK from its name in Bulgarian – *Natsionalen Dvorets na Kulturata*, see page 94) with its 3,800-seat main hall and many smaller concert spaces. Throughout the year, it hosts a variety of cultural events (see pages 9–11). Bulgaria Hall in Aksakov Street is home to the Bulgarian Philharmonic. The National Opera and Ballet performs in Vrabcha Street (see page 84). Tickets for ballet and

⬥ *Sofia City Garden, home to the National Theatre and Bulgaria Hall*

WHAT'S ON?

The *Insider's Guide* is a free listings magazine that appears every three months, and copies should be available in your hotel. There is also a free monthly *City Info Guide* that covers the same ground. Both these guides carry their own useful maps of the city area. Every Friday, the English-language *Sofia Echo* appears and carries current listings of what's on at the cinemas and details of theatrical and musical events.

See Ⓦ www.programata.bg for current information on Sofia's cultural, entertainment and nightlife scene.

music, which are amazingly affordable compared to Western Europe, can be booked in advance at the box offices of the various theatres. Usual opening hours are 10.00–18.30 (sometimes closed between 13.30 and 15.30).

Hollywood films, with subtitles in Bulgarian, are shown regularly in cinemas, and ticket prices average about €3. The main cinema complexes are **Cineplex** (ⓐ Arsenalski Blvd. 2 ❶ (02) 964 3007), with its nine screens at the City Center Sofia shopping mall (see page 110) and **Cinema City** (ⓐ Alexander Stamboliyski Blvd. 101 ❶ (02) 981 1911), with 12 screens and 3-D cinema in the Mall of Sofia (see page 22).

▶ *Alexander Stamboliyski, 1920s prime minister, outside the National Opera House*

Sport & relaxation

SPECTATOR SPORTS

Football Sofia's two biggest teams are the Bulgarian Army club team, **CSKA** (ⓦ www.cska.net), and **Levski** (ⓦ www.levski.bg). CSKA play at the Balgarska Armiya Stadium in Borisova Gradina Park (see page 104), which is where international fixtures are played. The other team, Levski, play at the Georgi Asparuhov Stadium in the northeast of

⬆ *Snowboarders waiting for the bus to Mount Vitosha*

the city. Tickets do not need to be bought in advance and are available at the grounds on the day of a match. Draw your own conclusions.

Balgarska Armiya Stadium ⓐ Borisova Gradina, south of Orlov Most ⓣ (02) 963 4279

Georgi Asparuhov Stadium ⓐ Suha Reka ⓣ (02) 847 8134

PARTICIPATION SPORTS

Skiing Mount Vitosha (see page 116) is only 22 km (13 1/2 miles) away from the city centre and reachable by a bus ride. Between December and April, thick snow cover provides good ski runs – with a total length of 29 km (18 miles) – that serve both beginners and the experienced. There is a ski school at Aleko, situated just above the tree line, that teaches absolute beginners from the age of six upwards, and all the gear can be hired by the day. Outside winter, the area is popular with hikers, and trails criss-cross the mountain. There is a chairlift from the village suburb of Dragalevtsi as well as the cable car from Simeonovo. On the more wooded western side of the mountain, Zlatni Mostove is an outdoor area that is a good picnic spot in the summer. If you go there on a weekday, you will have plenty of space to yourself and you can explore the huge boulders that line the course of the river.

Ten Pin Bowling There is a bowling alley in town at **Galaxy Bowling Club** (ⓐ Bulgaria Blvd. 1 ⓣ (02) 916 6590).

RELAXATION

Sofia has a number of parks, but the one that offers the most in the way of relaxation is Borisova Gradina (see page 104). This is the largest park in the city, and an hour or more could easily be spent wandering its paths; it is also suitable for jogging.

Accommodation

There is a good range of accommodation in Sofia, from hostels to 5-star opulence, and you should be able to stay close to the city centre. Some good, mid-range hotels, like the Lozenetz (see page 41), are just a little outside the city centre but still within walking distance – a tram ride or an inexpensive taxi-ride away. Expect some quirks as even the best hotels can fail when it comes to brown bread for breakfast, and a toaster may be missing from an otherwise good 3-star place. This sounds like carping, but prices are comparable to Western European ones where standards are higher.

It is best to make internet bookings in advance, either directly with the hotel or through an accommodation website like Ⓦ www.sofiahotels.net or Ⓦ www.hotelsinsofia.com. A buffet breakfast is included in the room rates. Tea- and coffee-making facilities are not usually available in hotel rooms, but mini-bars are in many mid-range hotels, and a safety deposit box is either in the room or available at reception. English-speaking staff in all the hotels listed here are usually very helpful when it comes to calling a taxi for you or dealing with day-to-day enquiries.

HOTELS

California £ Lovely place, a little outside the centre in Lozenets. A variety of rooms plus sauna, room service, internet access and a restaurant in traditional Bulgarian style. ❸ Bigla Street 30 ❶ (02) 962 9300 ❶ (02) 962 5542 Ⓦ www.hotelcaliforniasofia.com

Madrid £ Small hotel in a quiet street ten minutes' walking distance from the centre. The rooms are simply furnished but tidy and comfy. ❸ Dragovitsa Street 12 ❶ (02) 944 8952 ❶ (02) 943 3144 Ⓦ www.madridbg.com

PRICE CATEGORIES
The following price guides indicate the approximate cost of a room for two people for one night, including tax and breakfast unless otherwise stated.
£ up to €75   ££ €75–150   £££ over €150

Pop Bogomil £ Situated in an area of cobbled streets and close to the city centre. Rooms are smallish and decorated a little kookily, but are basically comfortable. Rooms with a bath need requesting in advance. ⊕ Pop Bogomil 5 ① (02) 983 1165 ⊕ (02) 983 7065 ⓦ www.bulgariabedandbreakfast.com

Tzar Asen £ Seven rooms in a quiet suburban setting. ⊕ Tsar Assen Street 68 ① (02) 954 7801 ⓦ www.hotel-tzar-asen.hit.bg

Legends £–££ Medium-sized, intimate hotel 3 km (nearly 2 miles) south of the centre, with convenient transport links to the city centre and very close to Hladilnika bus station for catching a bus to Vitosha. Reasonable prices for the stylish facilities and comfort. ⊕ Cherni Vrah Blvd. 56 ① (02) 961 7930 ⊕ (02) 961 7933 ⓦ www.hotel-legends.bg

Niky £–££ Quiet location off Vitosha Boulevard, with good-value singles and doubles plus 17 suites with kitchenettes. Free internet and pleasant restaurant. ⊕ Neofit Rilski Street 16 ① (02) 952 3058 ⊕ (02) 951 6091 ⓦ www.hotel-niky.com

Sveta Sofia £–££ Attractive and central location. ⊕ Pirotska Street 18 ① (02) 981 2634 ⊕ (02) 983 1723 ⓦ www.svetasofia-alexanders.com

Art 'Otel ££ One block away from Vitosha Boulevard, this hotel has over 20 rooms, some of which offer cityscape views. 🅐 Gladstone Street 44 ☎ (02) 980 6000 🅕 (02) 981 1909 🅦 www.artotel.biz

Arte ££ In the heart of Sofia, this offers stylish furnished rooms with flat-screen TVs and Wi-Fi. 🅐 Knyaz Dondukov Blvd. 5 ☎ (02) 402 7100 🅕 (02) 402 7109

Central ££ On the west side of the city, with 25 rooms that all have Wi-Fi. A bar, restaurant, sauna and laundry service feature among its attractions. 🅐 Hristo Botev Blvd. 52 ☎ (02) 981 2364 🅕 (02) 986 4561 🅦 www.central-hotel.com

Diter ££ A smart hotel in a quiet location with excellent facilities, including safe and mini-bar. Well managed; restaurant downstairs. 🅐 Han Asparuh 65 ☎ (02) 989 8998 🅦 www.diterhotel.com

🔺 *The Radisson SAS Grand Hotel is one of Sofia's top hotels*

Light ££ Located in a quiet, cobbled street, but central; a touch of class in the contemporary décor but most rooms have only a shower. ⓐ Veslets Street 37 ⓣ (02) 917 9090 ⓕ (02) 917 9010 ⓦ www.hotels.light.bg

Lozenetz ££ Just south of the city centre, this is a modern and classy hotel with a good restaurant, friendly staff and Wi-Fi connections. ⓐ Sveti Naum Blvd. 23 ⓣ (02) 965 4444 ⓕ (02) 965 4445 ⓦ www.lozenetzhotel.com

Central Park Hotel £££ Conveniently located just a few minutes away from the trendy shopping, eating and drinking zones and right in front of the National Palace of Culture. Bright rooms offering excellent views of Sofia's mountainous surroundings. Modern business centre and conference facilities. ⓐ Vitosha Blvd. 106 ⓣ (02) 805 8888 ⓕ (02) 805 8787 ⓦ www.centralparkhotel.bg

Hilton Hotel £££ Reliably first class, with free use of pool and gym, and a good restaurant; situated behind the NDK. ⓐ Bulgaria Blvd. 1 ⓣ (02) 933 5000 ⓕ (02) 933 5111 ⓦ www.sofia.hilton.com

Radisson SAS Grand Hotel £££ A great location opposite Alexander Nevsky Memorial Church, and one of the best places to stay. ⓐ Narodno Sabranie Sq. 4 ⓣ (02) 933 4334 ⓕ (02) 933 4335 ⓦ www.sofia.radissonsas.com

Sheraton Sofia Hotel Balkan £££ A landmark hotel when it opened in the mid-1950s, and now a classic with its high ceilings, marble columns and stately staircases. ⓐ Sveta Nedelya Sq. 5 ⓣ (02) 981 6541 ⓕ (02) 980 6464 ⓦ www.luxurycollection.com

APARTMENTS

Apartment House Dunav £–££ Fourteen fully furnished comfortable apartments decorated in neutral colours with equipped kitchenettes. Friendly and attentive staff. The rates fall substantially the longer you stay. ⓐ Dunav Street 38 ⓣ (02) 983 3002 ⓕ (02) 962 3804 ⓦ www.dunavapartmenthouse.com

HOSTELS

Be My Guest £ Dorms and double rooms spread about a funkily decorated hostel; good central location. ⓐ Ivan Vazov Street 13 ⓣ (02) 989 5092 ⓦ www.bemyguest-hostel.com

◗ *The elegant Sheraton Sofia*

HostelMostel £ Bunk-bed accommodation in dorms in a hostel with more living space than Be My Guest (see opposite). Popular hostel where floor space is also available if you have your own sleeping bag. **ⓐ** Makedonia Blvd. 2 **ⓣ** 0889 223296 **Ⓦ** www.hostelmostel.com

Internet Hostel £ In the heart of the city; nicely decorated, private rooms, decent kitchen, internet access. **ⓐ** Alabin Street 50A **ⓣ** 0888 384828 **ⓔ** interhostel@yahoo.co.uk

Kervan Hostel £ Comfortable and cosy hostel to the north of Alexander Nevsky Memorial Church and close to the Opera House. **ⓐ** Rositsa Street 3 **ⓣ** (02) 983 9428 **Ⓦ** www.kervanhostel.com

THE BEST OF SOFIA

Whether you're on a flying visit to Sofia or taking a more leisurely break in Bulgaria, the city offers sights and experiences that should not be missed.

TOP 10 ATTRACTIONS

- **Alexander Nevsky Memorial Church** Neo-Byzantine extravaganza and, outside, a great street market (see page 80)

- **Borisova Gradina** Sofia's largest park with ponds and paths and non-urban vibes (see page 104)

- **Boogying at the Bibliotekata** Underneath the National Library, there's live music... and a sushi bar. That's a library (see page 88)

- **Frescoes in Boyana Church** Unique frescoes from the 13th century, comparable to the achievements of the early Italian Renaissance (see page 106)

- **Rila Monastery** Bulgaria's best monastery – a day trip from Sofia (see page 130)

- **Sofia's pub-restaurants** A plethora of alfresco bars serving food through a long summer's night (see pages 26–31)

- **Women's Market** Balkan flavours in Sofia's most traditional market (see page 70)

- **Skiing and hiking around Mount Vitosha** The snow-capped mountain that can be seen from the city centre (see page 116)

- **Banya Bashi Mosque** The city's only functioning mosque has magnificent mineral baths (see page 66)

- **Sofia Synagogue** Spanish-Moorish style and, wait for it, the biggest chandelier in the Balkans (see page 69)

⬇ *Bulgarians and Russians meeting in victory, 1945*

Suggested itineraries

HALF-DAY: SOFIA IN A HURRY

There is enough time to walk the city centre and see the main sights. Start outside the Radisson SAS Grand Hotel (see page 41) and cross the cobbled square, past the white parliament building, to the Alexander Nevsky Memorial Church (see page 80) and its golden domes. The crypt houses a priceless collection of icons, while out in the public square vendors retail World War II memorabilia and assorted artefacts. A short walk westwards, along Tsar Osvoboditel Boulevard, passes the stunning little Russian Church (see page 83) and its five golden onion domes, then the National Art Gallery (see page 71) and the Ethnographic Museum (see page 71). They are on Alexander Batenberg Square, where troops once goose-stepped and tanks rolled by in convoys during the Stalinist era. Appropriately enough, you soon find yourself gazing up at the Party House (see page 66), former headquarters of the Communist Party. You are now on the west side of the city and close to Tsentralni Hali – an indoor market with a choice of places to eat (see page 75).

● *Parliament building*

1 DAY: TIME TO SEE A LITTLE MORE

The half-day itinerary above could be followed, after leaving Tsentralni Hali, by a visit to the city's attractive synagogue (see page 69) and then a stroll down the pedestrianised Pirotska Street, which leads to the Women's Market (see page 70). You may purchase very little, but the authentic flavour of the Balkans is gradually disappearing in the capital and it can still be experienced for real here. There is also time for a quick walk past the church of Sveta Nedelya (see page 69) and a look at the shops in Vitosha Boulevard. You could end the day in style by enjoying a Bulgarian-style meal at the fabulous Pod Lipite (see page 113) restaurant and taking a short stroll down to the live-music nightclub, Swingin' Hall (see page 114).

2–3 DAYS: TIME TO SEE A LOT MORE

The first day, or day-and-a-half, could be occupied with the suggestions above, while the extra time would allow for a day trip out of the city centre to the National History Museum (see page 109) or Boyana Church (see page 106). It takes only an hour to reach Mount Vitosha (see page 116), and you would also have time for a day's skiing or a hike on the mountain. The nights give you time to drop in on some more of the city's bars and restaurants.

LONGER: ENJOYING SOFIA TO THE FULL

You can do all of the above and still have time to experience the full Top 10 Attractions (see page 44). Spend a day exploring bucolic Koprivshtitsa (see page 136) and the town's traditional Bulgarian architecture (see page 12) and/or, in a more hedonistic spirit, take an excursion to the bars of Blagoevgrad. A trip to fortress-like Rila Monastery (see page 130) could also be on your itinerary.

Something for nothing

Sofia's great churches are free to enter and so you can explore Alexander Nevsky Memorial Church (see page 80), though there is a small charge to view the crypt. The National Gallery of Foreign Art (see page 84) is free on Mondays. The city's parks are free, and Borisova Gradina (see page 104) always makes a relaxing destination on a fine day. At the junction of Vitosha Boulevard and Patriarh Evtimii Boulevard, NDK Garden is not a very green space, and Sofia City Garden (see page 66) is a more peaceful place to take a rest; if you fancy your chess skills, feel free to challenge one of the players who regularly use part of the park.

Sofia has a compact city centre and the following walk costs nothing but takes in many sights. Start outside Sveta Nedelya Church (see page 69) and walk north up Maria Luiza Boulevard to Pirotska Street. Walk down pedestrianised Pirotska Street and at the end turn to the right to enter the Women's Market (see page 70). After exploring the market, retrace your steps to Maria Luiza Boulevard and cross to the other side, and head back the way you came. After passing the giant Tzum shopping mall (see page 74), turn left into Nezavisimost Square, and you immediately see the magisterial Party House (see page 66) looming ahead. Cross to the other side so that you keep Party House on your left as you walk into Alexander Batenberg Square and the City Garden (see page 66) on your right. There is a large open-air café-bar that opens in the summer opposite the **National Theatre** (❷ Ivan Vazov 5) in the park. After a rest in the park, walk back to Alexander Batenberg Square and, facing the park, the former royal palace that now houses the National Art Gallery (see page 71) and the National Ethnographic Museum (see page 71).

A short walk eastwards along Tsar Osvoboditel Boulevard brings you to the delightful St Nicholas Russian Church (see page 83). Continue along the boulevard until you come to the Radisson SAS Grand Hotel (see page 41) and Narodno Sabranie Square. From here you can see the Alexander Nevsky Memorial Church (see page 80) on your left. After leaving the church continue eastwards along Tsar Osvoboditel Boulevard and cross to the other side to see the Monument to the Soviet Army to admire the best example of communist sculpture in Sofia.

● *Frieze around the base of the Monument to the Soviet Army*

When it rains

All the churches and museums can be visited on a wet day and, as many of them are close to one another, you need only an umbrella to keep safely dry. From the Alexander Nevsky Memorial Church (see page 80) it takes less than five minutes to reach the Russian Church (see page 83). Almost next door, the National Art Gallery (see page 71) and the Ethnographic Museum (see page 71) are conveniently together in a former royal palace. Opposite the Russian Church there is a comfortable café to enjoy a break, and from the café it is a five-minute walk to the Archaeological Museum (see page 70). The Sofia Synagogue (see page 69), the Banya Bashi Mosque (see page 66) and the church of Sveta Nedelya (see page 69) are also near one another, and time inside these buildings could be combined with some window shopping in the Tzum shopping mall (see page 74) and, across the street, **Halite** (🅐 Maria Luiza Blvd.), where food and drink is also available.

A wet day provides an opportunity to visit some of the smaller museums and galleries dotted around the city. The foyer of the **Russian Cultural Centre** (🅐 Shipka 34 🕐 (02) 943 3065) is home to a virtually life-size model of the Vostok-3 capsule that sent Yuri Gagarin into space.

By way of entertainment, a visit to the cinema will escape the rain and the cinema complex, in the City Center Sofia shopping mall (see page 110), is a short walk from the rear of the Hilton Hotel (see page 41).

A trip to the National History Museum (see page 109) would take up at least half of one wet day although, to avoid the rain, a taxi ride there and back would be best. Whatever the weather, Sofia's countless bars are always open, and if you stayed in the vicinity of Tsar Ivan Shishman Street, it would be easy to pop from one to another without getting too wet.

🔺 *Dodge the rain showers at the Banya Bashi Mosque*

On arrival

TIME DIFFERENCE
Sofia is two hours ahead of Greenwich Mean Time (GMT) and seven hours ahead of Eastern Standard Time (EST).

ARRIVING
By air
Sofia International Airport (🕐 (02) 937 2211 🌐 www.sofia-airport.bg) is 10 km (7 miles) east of the city centre, consisting of two terminals with a shuttle between them. It is relatively small for a European capital but the basic facilities are provided: ATMs, bank offices, car hire counters, cafés and desks for booking a taxi. Ignore the taxi touts and, after using the ATM machine, book a taxi for the short journey into town. The fare will be between €5 and €7.50. Between 05.00 and 23.00, buses No 84 and No 284 run to Orlov Most, east of the city centre, from a bus stop outside the airport; you need to purchase a ticket (€0.25) from the kiosk near the bus stop before boarding the bus or from the bus driver (€0.50). If you have a lot of luggage, you have to buy separate tickets for every piece bigger than 60 x 60 x 40 cm (otherwise you could be fined).

By rail
Sofia's **Central Station** (🕐 (02) 931 1111 🌐 www.bdz.creato.biz) is an ugly concrete shelter north of the city centre on Maria Luiza Boulevard. It is 20 minutes away on foot or take tram Nos 1 or 7 to/from Sveta Nedelya Square (you should purchase your ticket from the kiosk before boarding). ATMs and left-luggage facilities are available at the station. Beware of meter scams from taxi drivers hanging around the station; it may be worth walking the short distance to the bus station and catching one there.

IF YOU GET LOST, TRY ...

Excuse me, do you speak English?
Извинете, говорите ли английски?
Izvinete, govorite li anglyski?

**Excuse me, is this the right way to... the cathedral/
the tourist office/the castle/the old town?**
Извинете, това ли е пътят за... катедралата/
туристическото бюро/замъка/стария град?
*Izvinete, tova li eh puhtyat za ... katedralata/
turisticheskoto byuro/zamuhka/stariya grad?*

Can you point to it on my map?
Може ли да ми покажете на моята карта?
Mozhe li da mi pokazhete na moyata karta?

By road

The **Central Bus Station** (📞 0900 21000 🌐 www.centralbusstation-sofia.com), 200 m (219 yds) east of the railway station on Maria Luiza Boulevard, is a well-organised place with good facilities, including ATMs, left-luggage facility, food court, information desk and a taxi-booking kiosk. For public transport into town, walk to the train station for tram Nos 1 or 7.

FINDING YOUR FEET

Sofia is a safe city to travel around and the pace of life is not frantic. The difficulty is grappling with the Cyrillic alphabet. Finding a menu

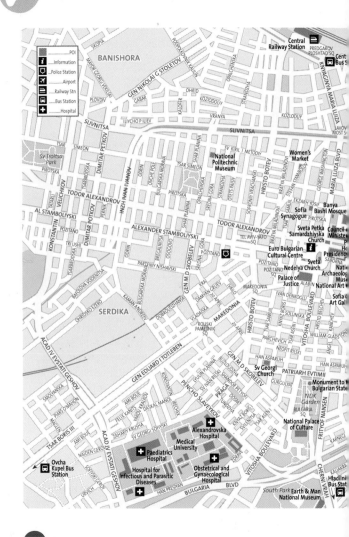

POI
Information
Police Station
Airport
Railway Stn
Bus Station
Hospital

BANISHORA

Central
Railway Station PREDGAROV
PLOSHTAD SQ

Cent
Bus S

SKOPIE

GEN GEORGI PEKLA

GEN NIKOLAI G STOLETOV

PODPOLKOVNIK KALITIN

RAVNIGNTA MARIA LUIZA

OHRID

DRAGOMAN

ORACHANSKA

STRANDZHA

PLOVDIV

CABAK

KOZLODUY

ILIYCHO P ILIEV

KOZLODUY

LAVOV
MOST S

SLIVNITSA

VRANYA

Sv Troitsa
Park

TSAR SIMEON

SLIVNITSA

SV KIRIL I METODIY

TSAR
SHARODSKA

DIMITAR PETKOV

SHAR PLANINA

National
Politechnic
Museum

Women's
Market

GEORGE WASHINGTON

VELICHKOV

PIROTSKA

ODRIN

OICHE POLE

TSAR SIMEON

OPALCHENSKA

SREDNA GORA

STRANDZHA

HRISTO BOTEV

BRATYA MILADINOVI

STEFAN STAMBOLOV

MARIA LUIZA BLVD

TODOR ALEXANDROV

INZH IVAN VANOV

BULGARSKA MORAVA

SOFRONIY VRACHANSKI

EKZARH YOSIF

Banya
Bashi Mosque

AL STAMBOLIYSKI

DIMITAR POTKOV

FERNI

PIROTSKA

Sofia
Synagogue

Sveta Petka
Samardzhiyska
Church

PIROTSKA

Council
Minister

KONSTANTIN

POZITANO

TRI USHI

SKARBODKA

ALEXANDER STAMBOLIYSKI

TEL AVIV-YAFO
SQ

TODOR ALEXANDROV

BRATYA MILADINOVI

P
He

SHARODKA

OSOGOVO

OPALCHENSKA

SRENA GORA

Euro Bulgarian
Cultural Centre

Presiden

National
Archaeolo
Muse

BREGALNITSA

GEN M D SKOBELEV

POZITANO

POZITANO
SQ

SABORNA

Sveta
Nedelya Church

ODRIN

PARTENIY NISHAVSKI

POZITANO

Palace of
Justice

ALABIN

National Art

Sofia (
Art Gal

KAMAN ANDREEV

BULGARSKA MORAVA

DOBROTOLHANSKI

MAKEDONIA
SQ

IVAN DENKOGLU

SERDIKA

KNAL

DAMYAN GRUEV

IVALO

MAKEDONIA

NEOFIT RILSKI

TSAR SAMUIL

BOLSINSKA

VITOSHA BOULEVARD

HRISTO BETCHER

BAYOVA VODENITSA

GHIROSKI EZERO

VOJDASKA

20 APRIL

ROUSKI
PAMETNIK
SQ

PARCHEVICH

HRISTO BOTEV

GEN BORIS

TSAR ASEN

WILLIAM GLADSTON

KANCHEV

ACAD IV EUSTATI GESHOV

GEN EDUARD I TOTLEBEN

USUN PLANINA

GEN M D SKOBELEV

HAN ASPARUH

HAN ASPARUH

SMOLYANSKA

BIARS OMAHON

KONSTANTIN

UGHEN PANINA

RILSKI

SV IVAN RILSKI

SHANDOR PETOFI

NUNDZHA

PATRIARH EVTIMII

Sv Georgi
Church

GURGULYAT

Monument to
Bulgarian State

TSAR BORIS III

AMI BOUE

FELIX KANITS

PENCHO SLAVEYKO

KRAKO

DASKAL MANOL

PRAGA

PIRIN

KNIAZ BORIS

TSAR ASEN

NDK
Garden

FRITJOF NANSEN

ACAD IV EUSTATI GESHOV

AMI BOUE

ZAHARY KRUSHA

SV GEORGI SOFIYSKI

Alexandrovska
Hospital

KNIAZ BORIS

SVILENTSA

BULGARIA
SQ

National Palace
of Culture

NAIDEN GEROV

Medical
University

DYAKON

KARNEZ

Ovcha
Kupel Bus
Station

SOFIYSKI GEROI

Paediatrics
Hospital

Hospital for
Infectious and Parasitic
Diseases

Obstetrical and
Gynaecological
Hospital

VITOSHA BOULEVARD

CHENRI VRAH

KAUARA

URICH

HAN PRESYAN

BULGARIA BLVD

South Park Earth & Man
National Museum

Hladilni
Bus Stat

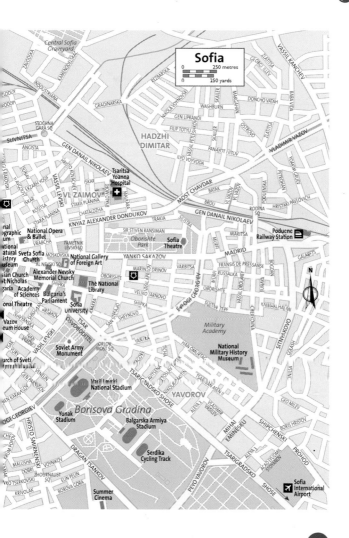

Sofia

0   250 metres
0   250 yards

in English is not difficult, but a sign or street name is more elusive, and it is good to have at least a nodding acquaintance with the alphabet.

THE CYRILLIC ALPHABET

Аа	a as in cat	Пп	p as in pot
Бб	b as in bus	Рр	r as in rasp
Вв	v as in very	Сс	s as in see
Гг	g as in go	Тт	t as in tip
Дд	d as in door	Уу	u as in rule
Ее	e as in bet	Фф	f as in fruit
Жж	zh like the s in leisure	Хх	ch as in loch
Зз	z as in zoo	Цц	ts as in shut
Ии	i as in bit	Чч	ch as in chip
Йй	y as in yes	Шш	sh as in ship
Кк	k as in kit	Щщ	sht like the last
Лл	l as in like		syllable in joshed
Мм	m as in met	Ъъ	u as in but
Нн	n as in net	Юю	yu as in you
Оо	o as in got	Яя	ya as in yarn

● РЕСТОРАНТ ГРОЗД = *RESTAURANT GROZD*

⬛ *Catch u trolleybus*

ORIENTATION

The use of the Cyrillic alphabet for street names makes orientation a little more difficult than it would otherwise be, and it pays to study a map before setting out for any destination. If you get confused about which street you are on, ask someone for directions – a young person is more likely to speak English – or enquire in a shop. The main tram routes, marked on the map, are often helpful in orientating yourself, and major landmarks include the National Palace of Culture (NDK, see page 94). Traffic drives on the right and usually stops for pedestrians at zebra crossings, but be careful and do not take this for granted.

GETTING AROUND

Trams, trolleybuses and regular buses criss-cross the city and are a reliable means of getting around if you know where to get off. Taxis

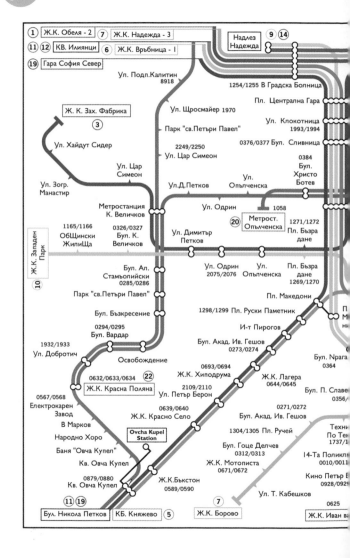

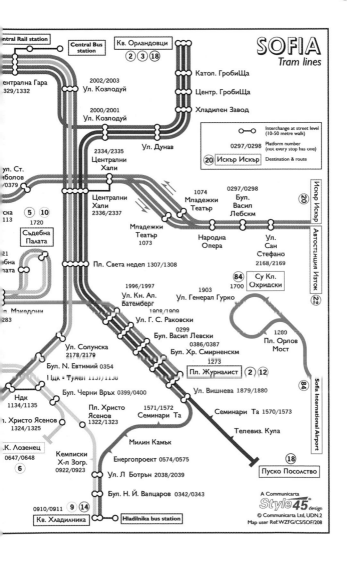

SOFIA
Tram lines

Central Rail station

Central Bus station

Кв. Орландовци
② ③ ⑱

Централна Гара
329/1332

Катол. ГробиЩа

Центр. ГробиЩа

2002/2003
Ул. Козлодуй

Хладилен Завод

2000/2001
Ул. Козлодуй

ул. Ст.
аболов
0379

Ул. Дунав

2334/2335
Центральни
Хали

Младежки
Театър

0297/0298
Бул.
Васил
Лебскм

Искър Искър
⑳

ка
113

⑤ ⑩
1720

Съдебна
Палата

Централни
Хали
2336/2337

1074

Автостанция Изток

21
ебна
лата

Младежки
Театър
1073

Пл. Света недел 1307/1308

Народна
Опера

Ул.
Сан
Стефано
2168/2169

1996/1997
Ул. Кн. Ал.
Батемберг

1903
Ул. Генерал Гурко

⑧④
1700

Су Кл.
Охридски

Interchange at street level
(10-50 metre walk)

0297/0298 Platform number
(not every stop has one)

⑳ Искър Искър Destination & route

n Македони
283

1908/1909
Ул. Г. С. Раковски

0299
Бул. Васил Левски

0386/0387
Бул. Хр. Смирненскм

1289
Пл. Орлов
Мост

Ул. Солунска
2178/2179

1273

Пл. Журналист ② ⑫

⑧④

Бул. N. Евтимий 0354

Ндк = Тунел 1137/1138

Ул. Вишнева 1879/1880

Sofia International Airport

Ндк
1134/1135

Бул. Черни Връх 0399/0400

Семинари Та 1570/1573

р. Христо Ясенов
1324/1325

Пл. Христо
Ясенов
1322/1323

1571/1572
Семинари Та

Телевиз. Кула

Милин Камък

.К. Лозенец
0647/0648
⑥

Кемписки
Х-л Зогр.
0922/0923

Енергопроект 0574/0575

⑱

Пуско Посолство

Ул. Л Ботрън 2038/2039

A Communicarta
Style 45 design
© Communicarta Ltd, UDN.2
Map user Ref:WZFG/CS/SOF/208

Бул. Н. Й. Вапцаров 0342/0343

0910/0911 ⑨ ⑭

Кв. Хладилника

Hladilnika bus station

are plentiful and inexpensive and can be booked in advance. Best of all, the city centre is small and compact enough to get around mostly on foot, and this is by far the most enjoyable option. There is one metro line, serving the western suburb of Lyulin, but you are very unlikely to ever need to travel there. There are also private minibuses that drop passengers off at any point along their set route, but unless you know the route you are also unlikely to use this means of transport.

The city's trams and buses are often old and none too clean and chug along slowly at times, but services are reliable and run from around 05.00 to 23.30. Tickets need to be purchased before boarding and they are validated on the tram or bus by inserting them into one of the mechanical puncher machines positioned near the doors. Single-journey tickets cost €0.35, but a strip of ten tickets costs €3 and saves time and money; with a strip of ten the rule is that they must be used in sequence and those numbered one to nine are not valid unless you still have the tenth, un-punched one, in your possession. Travel passes are also available: for one day they're €2.50; and for one month €18.50. Tickets are purchased from kiosks, often the ones selling newspapers, near bus stops. The challenge, though, is to find the bus or tram stop because they are often unmarked and you may have to look for likely groups of passengers waiting for a bus. Tram stops are sometimes in the middle of the road and passengers wait on the pavement until the tram approaches.

Registered taxis, painted bright yellow, are easy to find and use digital meters. There are disreputable taxi companies that will overcharge, but as long as you use the companies listed here there should be no problem. Oval sticker on the windscreen, driver's ID card, car number and table of fares should be clearly displayed, but most drivers do not speak English. Taxis can be booked in advance

🔺 *A tram passes through the cobbled streets of Sofia*

● *Ask your hotel staff if you need help with transportation*

and reception staff at your hotel are usually happy to call one for
you and, if necessary, explain to the driver where you want to go.
Three reliable taxi companies are:

OK Supertrans ❶ (02) 973 2121
Taxi S Express ❶ (02) 912 80
Radio CB Taxi ❶ (02) 912 63

CAR HIRE
Car hire is hardly worth the trouble of organising when public
transport serves the excursion destinations, although a car would be
helpful for Rila Monastery (see page 130). **Avis** (Ⓦ www.avis.bg) and
Hertz (Ⓦ www.hertz.bg) have offices at the airport and in the city.

▶ *The rooftops of Sofia*

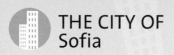

Around Sveta Nedelya Square

Sveta Nedelya can be regarded as the centre of the city and a major orientation point when you first start exploring it. It is a compact area and everywhere can be reached on foot. Vitosha Boulevard, the main shopping street, runs due south from the square, while immediately to the north stands the landmark Monument to Holy Wisdom. The main way east leads almost immediately to Nezavisimost Square, also known as the Largo, and this leads to the attractions on the east side of the city. The main street heading north from Sveta Nedelya Square is Maria Luiza Boulevard and it heads towards the bus and railway station. Although Maria Luiza Boulevard accesses some sights, principally the synagogue (see page 69), it is not long before this street becomes decidedly grotty and the way to the bus and railway stations becomes one of the least attractive thoroughfares in the city.

SIGHTS & ATTRACTIONS

Alexander Batenberg Square

The square near the Party House used to be called the Ninth of September Square, commemorating the date of the Communist takeover in 1944, and it was the focal point for government-related parades until 1989. There used to be a giant mausoleum facing the square, holding the embalmed body of Georgi Dimitrov, the country's first Communist leader. The Bulgarian politburo would stand on the mausoleum to take the salute from goose-stepping troops and the convoys of tanks that rolled by over the cobbles. Dynamite removed the mausoleum in 2000, but ideas for replacing the site with something attractive were not followed through and dull shrubbery covers the ground.

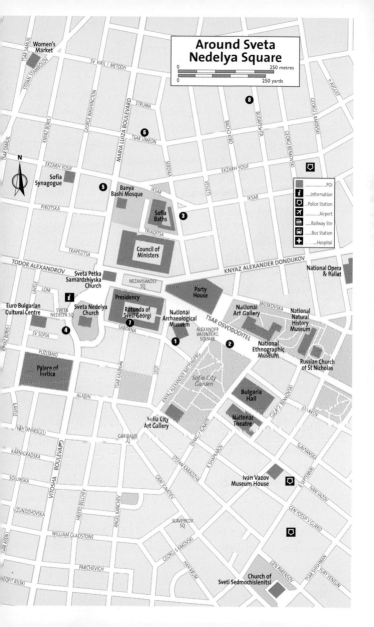

Around Sveta Nedelya Square

0 ————— 250 metres
0 ————— 250 yards

Women's Market

TSAR SAMUIL
STEFAN STAMBOLOV
SV. KIRIL I METODIY
STRUMA
GEORGI RAKOVSKI
KNYAZ BORIS
GEORGE WASHINGTON
MARIA LUIZA BOULEVARD
BACHO KIRO
BUDAPESTA
GEORGI BENKOVSKI
❽
TSAR SIMEON ❻
EKZARH YOSIF
SEROIKA
VESLETS
EKZARH YOSIF
Sofia Synagogue
❺ Banya Bashi Mosque
IKSAR
IKSAR
Sofia Baths ❸
PIROTSKA
TRAPEZITSA
TRIADITSA
Council of Ministers

POI
ⓘ ....Information
Ⓟ ....Police Station
✈ ....Airport
🚆 ....Railway Stn
🚌 ....Bus Station
➕ ....Hospital

TODOR ALEXANDROV
Sveta Petka Samardzhiyska Church
LAVELE
LOM
NEZAVISIMOST SQ
KNYAZ ALEXANDER DONDUKOV
National Opera & Ballet
Euro Bulgarian Cultural Centre
ⓘ SVETA NEDELYA SQ
Presidency
Party House
MOSKOVSKA
National Art Gallery
National Natural History Museum
KNYAZ BORIS
Sveta Nedelya Church
Rotunda of Sveti Georgi ❼
National Archaeological Museum ❶
TSAR OSVOBODITEL
SABORNA
SV SOFIA
ALEXANDER BATENBERG
ALEXANDER BATENBERG SQUARE
National Ethnographic Museum ❷
Russian Church of St Nicholas
PUZITANO
Palace of Justice
ALABIN
TSAR KALOYAN
LEGE
Sofia City Garden
Bulgaria Hall
GRAF IGNATIEV
SLAVYANSKA
LAVELE
IVAN DENKOGLU
KNYAZ ALEXANDER BATENBERG
National Theatre
RAKOVSKI
KARNIGRADSKA
VITOSHA BOULEVARD
Sofia City Art Gallery
DYAKON IGNATIY
STEFAN KARADZHA
K SHAPKAREV
SOLUNSKA
HRISTO BELCHEV
ANGEL KANCHEV
GARIBALDI
UZUNDZHOVSKA
GRAF GALERY
Ivan Vazov Museum House Ⓟ
6 SEPTEMVRI
IVAN VAZOV
WILLIAM GLADSTONE
SLAVEYKOV SQ
GEORGI S RAKOVSKI
HAN KRUM
Ⓟ
GEN YOSSIFF GURKO
GEN PARENSOV
DENKOGLU
PARCHEVICH
TSAR SISHMAN
TSAR VENELIN
NEOFIT RILSKI
Church of Sveti Sedmochislenitsi

N

Banya Bashi Mosque

The only city mosque still in use, this takes its name from the nearby mineral baths (banya bashi means 'many baths') and dates back to the 16th century. The architect was Hadji Mimar Sinan, the leading Muslim designer of the age and creator of some magnificent edifices outside Bulgaria, but on this project he contented himself with a single large dome and one minaret. Notwithstanding the modesty of the design, the mosque is a singularly attractive addition to the city centre. The mineral baths to the rear of the mosque were built in the early 20th century and rate as one of the architectural highlights of the city. ⓐ Maria Luiza Blvd. 🕓 08.00–17.00 ⓘ Visitors welcome except at prayer times, expect least access on Fridays; women should be modestly dressed

Party House

A short walk around the corner from the Balkan Sheraton on to Nezavisimost Square immediately brings into view the Party House, the large, neoclassical building that was once the headquarters of the country's Communist Party. The building looks powerful, and was even more so when it sported a giant red star on its summit. The star was removed in August 1990 when protestors tried to set it on fire. ⓐ Nezavisimost Sq.

Sofia City Garden

Immediately south of Alexander Batenberg Square, the pretty stretch of green that constitutes Sofia City Garden comes into its own with the advent of spring. Local office workers take advantage of the sunshine during their breaks, and chess players settle into studied silence after setting their game clocks. There is more than one place serving drinks and the elegant neoclassical façade of the

⬥ *National Theatre, Sofia City Garden*

⬤ *Ceremony preparation in the beautiful Sveta Nedelya orthodox church*

National Theatre (see page 48) bestows an air of cultural refinement on the park scene. ⓐ South of Alexander Batenberg Sq. 🕐 24 hours

Sofia Synagogue

Designed and built in the first decade of the 20th century, this elegant and imaginative synagogue is a reminder that at one time one in five of the city's citizens were Jews and respected highly enough to add their cultural contribution to the skyline of the city centre. The Austrian architect and designer Friedrich Gruenager boldly mixed Moorish and Byzantine features around a large octagonal dome and multiple turrets. The interior is a delightful surprise with art nouveau-style decorations and a giant brass chandelier weighing over 2,000 kg (4,410 lb). Built to house 1,300, attendances now number less than 75; the city's Jews mostly emigrated to Palestine in the late 1940s.
ⓐ Ekzarh Yosif Street 🕿 (02) 983 1273 🕸 www.sofiasynagogue.com
🕐 08.30—16.30 Mon—Fri, Sat am for services, closed Sun; ring the bell for the caretaker; there's a small charge for depositing any bags

Sveta Nedelya Church

The present church in Sveta Nedelya Square occupies a spot where a succession of churches has stood since medieval times. The location is associated with a Serbian king, Stefan Urish, whose bones are believed to have the power to perform miracles and are preserved in a wooden box to the right of the iconostasis. The church you see today was built in the mid-19th century, and in 1925 it survived a bombing attempt to eliminate the Bulgarian royal family, who were in the church attending a funeral. Although the building was badly damaged and over 100 mourners killed, the royals escaped unhurt. ⓐ Sveta Nedelya Sq. 🕿 (02) 987 5748 🕐 07.00—19.00; daily liturgy at 08.30 and 16.00

PIROTSKA STREET AND WOMEN'S MARKET

Pirotska Street, one block south of the street where Sofia Synagogue stands (see page 69), is a pleasant pedestrianised street with small shops occupying old buildings that date back a century or more. At the end of this street, a right turn at the junction where trams cross leads directly to the Women's Market, or Zhenski Pazar, a dense but not claustrophobic open-air bazaar. Farmers sell their fresh produce alongside stalls retailing inexpensive clothing, broomsticks for the home and assorted items. The market has atmosphere and a character that is quite at odds with the air of sophistication being promoted in the rest of the city. ⓐ Pirotska Street and Stefan Stambolov Street ⓛ Women's Market: 08.00–19.00

Sveta Petka Samardzhiyska Church

Situated in the subway next to the Sheraton Hotel (it wasn't found until the end of World War II), this is one of the few medieval churches in Sofia to have survived to the present day. Samardzhiyska means 'of the saddlemakers', and this is apt as this is where such craftsmen used to hold their rituals. ⓐ Nezavisimost Sq. ⓛ 09.00–17.00

CULTURE

National Archaeological Museum

A modest but engaging collection of Thracian, Greek and Roman remains and some medieval artefacts from around the country. The more spectacular exhibits include a Thracian gold burial mask from the fourth century BC that was excavated in 2004. There is also a grave stone from the sixth century BC, found at the site of an ancient Greek colony on the Black Sea coast. Directly across the cobbled street from the museum's entrance are the offices of the Bulgarian president. The entrance is fronted by guards in fancy 19th-century dress, and on the hour they do a quick pirouette routine. ⓐ Saborna Street 2 ⓣ (02) 988 2406 ⓦ http://aim.sofianet.net ⓛ 10.00–18.00 Tues–Sun, closed Mon. Admission charge

National Art Gallery

The other half of the former royal palace housing the Ethnographic Museum constitutes the National Art Gallery. The galleries downstairs are devoted to temporary exhibitions of contemporary Bulgarian art, the quality of which varies, while the main galleries use their space to good effect in highlighting the best Bulgarian artists of the past. Look for the work of Vladimir Dimitrov-Maistora (1882–1960), Bulgaria's greatest artist of the 20th century. His paintings of peasant girls in bucolic settings are strangely alluring because of a near-mystical quality endowed by the colours. ⓐ Alexander Batenberg Sq. 1 ⓣ (02) 980 3325 ⓛ 10.00–18.00 Tues–Sun, closed Mon. Admission charge

National Ethnographic Museum

Reflecting Bulgarian culture through the centuries, the collections of Balkan arts and crafts that make up this museum are housed in one half of the former royal palace and this explains why features of the building's interior design, the plasterwork especially, are themselves an attraction of any visit. The particular theme behind a special exhibition that is showcased while you are in the city may help you to decide whether to make a visit or not. Unlike some of the city museums, the exhibits are all explained in English. ⓐ Alexander Batenberg Sq. 1 ⓣ (02) 987 4191 ⓛ 10.00–18.00 Tues–Sun, closed Mon. Admission charge

Rotunda of Sveti Georgi
Easy to miss, tucked away behind the Sheraton Sofia Balkan Hotel, Sofia's oldest church stands in a small courtyard. The red-brick exterior looks uninspiring and only its fourth-century Roman origins would seem to impart significance to the building, but step inside to view some stunning 14th-century frescoes and a depiction of wise men that dates from the 10th and 12th centuries. The church became a mosque during the Ottoman period, and the frescoes,

◆ *The Rotunda of Sveti Georgi*

painted over, remained hidden until the 20th century. 🄰 Sveta
Nedelya Sq. 2 🄱 08.00–17.00

Sofia City Art Gallery

Constantly changing profiles of either contemporary Bulgarian artists
or international shows; the information sheets are not in English but
with free admission you have nothing to lose by popping in to view
the works. 🄰 Gurko Street 1 🄱 (02) 987 2181 🅆 www.sghg.cult.bg
🄱 10.00–19.00 Tues–Sat, 11.00–17.00 Sun, closed Mon

RETAIL THERAPY

Bulgarski Dyukyan A cornucopia of kitchenware that sells Balkan crockery, embroidered tablecloths and peasant-style copper pots. ⓐ Pirotska Street 11 ⓛ 09.30–19.30 Mon–Fri, 10.00–17.00 Sat, closed Sun

Ethnographic Museum Shop Bulgarian kilims are one of the better buys, but there's also jewellery, folk artefacts and Bulgarian music. You do not need to visit the museum to check out the shop (which, incidentally, also opens on Mondays, when the museum itself is closed). ⓐ Alexander Batenberg Sq. 1 ⓣ (02) 987 4191 ⓛ 10.00–18.00

Stenata To find this shop, walk west along Pozitano Street from Sveta Nedelya Square, and Bratya Miladinovi Street is on your left. Stenata's stock of hiking, camping and climbing gear is the best in the city. ⓐ Bratya Miladinovi Street 5 ⓣ (02) 980 5491 ⓦ www.stenata.com ⓛ 10.00–19.00 Mon–Fri, 10.00–18.00 Sat, closed Sun

Tzum Once the consumer showpiece of Communist-era Sofia, now fulfilling a similar function for the post-Communist bourgeoisie of the city: three levels of boutiques, accessories, cosmetics and foreign newspapers. There's also a café and restaurant. ⓐ Maria Luiza Blvd. 2 ⓣ (02) 926 0700 ⓦ www.tzum.bg ⓛ 09.00–22.00 Mon–Sat, 10.00–20.00 Sun

TAKING A BREAK

Art Club Museum £ ❶ Tucked away at the back of the Archaeological Museum and attracting a sophisticated-looking set of customers,

this is an ideal spot for coffee and cakes or something more substantial from a menu of salads and pasta dishes; no smoking in the downstairs section where the seating rubs shoulders with ancient gravestones.
ⓐ Saborna Street 2 ❶ (02) 980 6664 🕒 24 hours

Bulgaria £ ❷ A very swish café, carpeted, with large glass windows for street-watching. Have a posh frappé or Viennese coffee with helpings of tiramisu, strudel or blackberry pie. The truffle and white chocolate also tempts the palate. ⓐ Tsar Osvoboditel Blvd. 4
❶ (02) 988 5307 🕒 08.00–22.00

Classic £ ❸ This pizza restaurant is located just five minutes' walk from Sveta Nedelya Square in a tiny street near the Party House. The simple (but pleasant) interior, a reliable range of pizzas and salads, friendly service and Wi-Fi make it great for a break.
ⓐ Serdika Street 14 ❶ 0878 656401 🕒 11.00–00.00

Happy Bar & Grill £ ❹ The interior décor: neon-lit guitars alongside rock and movie posters on the walls, and laminated menus; a bright and cheerful joint for drinks or a quick meal from the menu of grills, chicken and countless salads. There's another branch at Rakovski Street 145. ⓐ Sveta Nedelya Sq. 4 ❶ (02) 980 7353 🕒 24 hours

Tsentralni Hali £ ❺ On the top floor of this restored market hall there is a food court with various options or, in the basement, a branch of the always-reliable Trops Kushta. ⓐ Maria Luiza Blvd. 25
❶ (02) 917 6111 🕒 07.00–00.00

L'Etranger ££ ❻ An intimate restaurant that offers delicious dishes, perfectly prepared and arranged by the French chef. The desserts are

real gems. ⓐ Tsar Simeon Street 78 ❶ (02) 983 1417 🕐 12.00–22.00
Mon–Fri, 18.00–22.00 Sat, closed Sun

AFTER DARK

RESTAURANTS

Kumbare ££ ❼ Everything you could expect from a Greek restaurant
– plenty of grilled lamb and fish dishes accompanied by abundant
salads, all prepared under the watchful eye of a head chef from Tassos.
The chandeliers and Ionian columns only add to the Mediterranean
vibe. ⓐ Saborna Street 14 ❶ (02) 981 1749 🕐 11.00–00.00

◗ *Upstairs at Sin City*

Otvad Aleyata Zad Shkafa £££ ❶ One of the most elegant and atmospheric restaurants in Sofia. The menu is a tad extravagant for some, but all the dishes are delicious and look like real works of art. Excellent service, too. ⓐ Budapeshta Street 31 ❶ (02) 983 5545 ❶ 12.00–00.00

NIGHTLIFE

Gramofon Flashing lights, loud music, big dance floor and stylish clientele are the main features of the club. The menu offers a dazzling array of cocktails for all tastes and price ranges. ⓐ Budapeshta Street 6 ❶ (02) 981 1410 ❶ 24 hours

Sin City The city's biggest entertainment complex, consisting of pop-folk, house and retro music halls as well as a piano bar and café. Modern flashy interiors and high-quality sound systems. ⓐ Hristo Botev Blvd. 61 ❶ (02) 810 8888 ❶ 21.00–06.00. Admission charge

Toba & Co Tucked away to the rear of the National Art Gallery is this odd little joint that turns into a swinging venue when the right kind of DJ is on the decks. ⓐ Moskovska Street 6 ❶ (02) 989 4996 ❶ 10.00–03.00

Around Alexander Nevsky Memorial Church

Immediately north of Tsar Osvoboditel Boulevard is Alexander Nevsky
Memorial Church (see page 80). Tsar Osvoboditel Boulevard itself leads
to Narodno Sabranie Square, another landmark location for orientation
purposes, identified by the curving façade of the Radisson SAS Grand
Hotel (see page 41). Tsar Shishman Street, the first turning on the left
with your back to the entrance of the Radisson, is an important street
for accessing bars, restaurants and shops in this area.

SIGHTS & ATTRACTIONS

Graf Ignatiev Street

Graf Ignatiev Street is an extremely busy – by Sofia's standards –
tram-laden thoroughfare that cuts across the city centre from near
Sveta Nedelya Square towards the southeastern outskirts of the
capital. It is named in honour of the Russian count, who was the
grandfather of the novelist Michael Ignatiev. Graf Ignatiev was
instrumental in getting Tsar Alexander III to take on the Ottoman
Empire and thus liberate Bulgaria. Graf Ignatiev Street goes across
Slaveikov Square where there are a number of bookshops and open-
air bookstalls, before it becomes part of one of the city's main fruit
and vegetable markets. At the point where Graf Ignatiev Street meets
Tsar Shishman Street, which runs northeast up to the Radisson SAS
Grand Hotel, stands the church of Sveti Sedmochislenitsi.

Narodno Sabranie Square

Tsar Osvoboditel Boulevard connects Sveta Nedelya Square in the
west of the city with Narodno Sabranie Square (National Assembly
Square) in the east. This large cobbled area is defined on its north

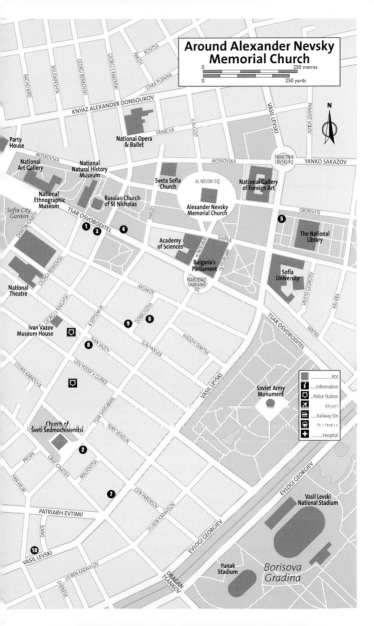

Around Alexander Nevsky Memorial Church

0   250 metres
0   250 yards

N

KNYAZ ALEXANDER DONSOUKOV

Party House

National Art Gallery

National Natural History Museum

National Opera & Ballet

Sveta Sofia Church

AL NEVSKI SQ

National Gallery of Foreign Art

YANKO SAKAZOV

PAMETNIK LEVSKI SQ

MOSKOVSKA

VASIL LEVSKI

PANIOT VOLOV

National Ethnographic Museum

Russian Church of St Nicholas

Alexander Nevsky Memorial Church

Sofia City Garden

TSAR OSVOBODITEL

① **③** **④**

OBORISHTE

⑤

The National Library

Academy of Sciences

Bulgaria's Parliament

SHIPKA

Sofia University

National Theatre

NARODNO SABRANIE SQ

AKSAKOV

TSAR OSVOBODITEL

Ivan Vazov Museum House

☒

IVAN VAZOV

⑨ **⑥**

SLAVYANSKA

HADZHI DIMITAR

⑧

GEN YOSSIEF GURGO

VASIL LEVSKI

☒

Soviet Army Monument

Church of Sveti Sedmochislenitsi

②

EVLOGI GEORGIEV

⑦

Vasil Levski National Stadium

PATRIARH EVTIMII

⑩

VASIL LEVSKI

EVLOGI GEORGIEV

DRAGAN TSANKOV

Yunak Stadium

Borisova Gradina

	POI
i	Information
☒	Police Station
✈	Airport
▤	Railway Stn
▥	Bus Station
✚	Hospital

ALEXANDER NEVSKY MEMORIAL CHURCH

Russian architects, principally Alexander Pomerantsev from St Petersburg, designed this church in the 1880s (building was completed in 1924), with the conscious aim of emulating the architectural glory of Byzantium. They undoubtedly succeeded because the result is a masterpiece that magnificently balances multiple gold-leafed domes to create an aesthetically pleasing structure. It was built to commemorate Russia's costly contribution to Bulgaria's liberation – countless thousands of Russians died fighting in the 1877–8 War of Liberation – and the money was raised by public subscriptions. The name of the church, however, refers to the subject of Eisenstein's famous film, a 13th-century prince who helped preserve Novgorod's independence.

The atmospheric interior is generously decorated with dynamic frescoes illuminated by numerous candles flickering in the darkness and enriched by onyx and alabaster columns adorning the thrones in the iconostasis. ⓐ Alexander Nevsky Sq. ⓣ (02) 988 1704 ⓒ 07.00–19.00; daily prayers: 08.00 and 17.00; vigil: 18.30 Sat. Mass: 09.30 Sun

side by the country's parliament building and, facing it on the south side in front of the Radisson SAS Grand Hotel, a 14-m (46-ft) monument depicting Tsar Alexander II of Russia on horseback. The tsar is honoured because it was his declaration of war on the Ottoman Empire that led to Bulgarian independence. Those who actually did the fighting are represented in the reliefs around the pedestal.

ⓞ *Alexander Nevsky Memorial Church with a sprinkling of snow*

🔺 Golden domes of the Russian Church of St Nicholas

National Natural History Museum

An absolute treat, this, especially for children. The museum, which is not very catchily known locally as the NMNHS, houses a great collection of fossils and mammals, hundreds of species of birds and thousands of insects. OK, most of them are stuffed and pickled, but there are also many live reptiles. A small gift shop sells fantastic souvenirs, in the form of minerals and fossils. ⓐ Tsar Osvoboditel Blvd. 1 ❶ (02) 987 4195 ⏱ 10.00–18.00. Admission charge

Russian Church of St Nicholas

The Russian theme continues with this highly photogenic and spirited creation gracing Tsar Osvoboditel Boulevard. The green steeple and the perfectly proportioned golden onion domes create an effervescence that is cheerfully at odds with the dour concrete that makes up so many of the buildings on this thoroughfare. The church was built in the early 20th century to serve the city's Russian elite and would not look out of place in the Kremlin. The interior is dark and mysterious, filled with the scent of burning candles and incense. ⓐ Tsar Osvoboditel Blvd. 3 ❶ (02) 986 2715 ⏱ 08.30 18.30

Sveta Sofia Church

Sitting in the shadow of Alexander Nevsky Memorial Church (see page 80), this brown brick church is the second-oldest building in Sofia, and it's had a fascinating life. Constructed on the site of a Roman theatre, its first incarnation was as a fifth-century basilica. During Ottoman rule, the church was converted into a mosque and the original 12th-century frescoes were destroyed. After the 1878 liberation, it was restored and reinstated as a church. Outside, to the left of the main entrance, stands the Monument to the Unknown

Soldier, lit by a perpetual flame in honour of those who died for Bulgaria. ⓐ Parizh Street 2 ⓣ (02) 987 0971 ⓛ 09.00–18.00

CULTURE

Crypt of Alexander Nevsky Memorial Church

The unrivalled collection of icons in the church's crypt is from all parts of the country, a result of scouring obscure churches and isolated monasteries, and covering almost a millennium in time. The majority of icons date from the last two centuries; the rarest are unique examples of medieval iconography; and a common pictorial theme is of the warrior saints George and Demetrius slaying dragons – a coded representation of the struggle against Ottoman oppression. ⓐ Entrance to the left of the church doors in Alexander Nevsky Sq. ⓣ (02) 981 5775 ⓛ 10.00–17.30 Tues–Sun, closed Mon. Admission charge

National Gallery of Foreign Art

Eclectic is the best way to describe what is on show, and the chances are that you will find something surprising and rewarding. The Asian art from Burma and Japan makes up the most gratifying exhibits for many visitors. Minor European art includes a Picasso lithograph, drawings by Delacroix and Renoir, and a bewitching piece by Franz von Stick. The basement contains a fourth-century Roman tomb. ⓐ Alexander Nevsky Sq. 1 ⓣ (02) 988 4922 ⓦ www.ngfa.icb.bg ⓛ 11.00–18.00 Wed–Mon, closed Tues. Admission charge, but free on Mon

National Opera and Ballet

Built in 1909 and seating 1,200, this is the city's leading venue for operas and ballets. Some operas are sung in Bulgarian and some

in Italian, so check beforehand to find out what's being staged.
ⓐ Vrabcha Street 1 ⓣ Ticket office (02) 987 1366 ⓛ 09.30–18.30
Mon–Fri, 10.30–18.00 Sat & Sun

RETAIL THERAPY

Alexander Nevsky Square Market A not-to-be-missed flea market
selling World War II and Communist-era memorabilia, stamps,
postcards, coins, medals and assorted bric-à-brac. Very little schlock,
apart from the cheaply lacquered Russian dolls and the array of
reproduction icons. Cross the square to the eastern side for women
selling embroidered lace, cardigans and tablecloths. ⓐ Alexander
Nevsky Sq. ⓛ 09.00–18.00

Art Gallery Paris Art Gallery Paris is a small, owner-run gallery
selling original work by a new generation of unknown Bulgarian
artists specialising in figurative and expressive art. Parizh Street
runs along the west side of Alexander Nevsky Memorial Church
and the shop is near the National Opera House. ⓐ Parizh Street 8
ⓣ (02) 980 8093 ⓦ www.gallery-paris.com ⓛ 11.00–18.30 Mon–Fri,
11.00–17.00 Sat, closed Sun

Cheers Three outlets in this part of the city with good selections of
Bulgarian wines and spirits. ⓐ Vasil Levski Blvd. 59 ⓣ (02) 987 1252
ⓐ Tsar Osvoboditel Blvd. 14 ⓣ (02) 986 1856 ⓐ Rakovski Street 116
ⓣ (02) 981 2729 ⓦ www.cheers.bg ⓛ 09.00–22.00 Mon–Sat,
10.00–21.00 Sun

Grita Gallery Alongside the paintings in which this gallery majors,
you'll see many an item of sculpture and other, more esoteric, forms

of art. It's always worth a visit as turnover is high, and you never know what delights will be sitting coyly in the window. ⓐ Vrabcha Street 14 ⓣ 0887 769392 ⓛ 11.00–19.00 Mon–Fri, 11.00–17.00 Sat, closed Sun

Mirela Bratova Bratova, the designer who makes the clothes you see in this one-off boutique, works with linen and silk to produce trousers, jackets and suits for women and some lovely tops using Thai silk. One of the more original designers in Sofia. ⓐ Tsar Shishman Street 4 ⓣ (02) 980 7156 ⓛ 10.30–20.00 Mon–Fri, 10.30–18.00 Sat, closed Sun

Nataly Extravagant clothes made by the top Bulgarian designer Nataly Genova, alongside locally produced designer jewellery, hand-painted silk scarves and other fashionable accessories. ⓐ Gurko Street 38 ⓣ (02) 980 7603 ⓛ 10.30-19.00 Mon–Sat, closed Sun

Noe Gallery Original Bulgarian artwork – paintings, wood and bronze carvings – of some quality. You could engage in a little gentle bargaining, though prices are reasonable. ⓐ Vrabcha Street 12A ⓣ (02) 980 6941 ⓦ www.gallerynoe.com ⓛ 12.00–18.30 Mon–Sat, closed Sun

Pretty Things Workshop A delightful shop offering a wide range of beautiful hand-made souvenirs, gifts, home decorations and bedding. ⓐ Krakra Street 12 ⓣ (02) 943 8220 ⓛ 10.00–20.00 Mon–Fri, 11.00–18.00 Sat, closed Sun

TAKING A BREAK

Devette Drakona £ ❶ An essential for fans of Chinese food, with wonderful views of the magnificent Russian Church of St Nicholas

THE BEST MARKET IN SOFIA

For antiques of the kind that will fit easily into your luggage there is nowhere more tempting than the market immediately north of the Alexander Nevsky Memorial Church. World War II items range from German helmets and medals to submarine stopwatches, and one trader does a nice line in Soviet-era hip flasks carrying KGB insignia (or are these just clever fakes?).

● *Varied items are on offer at a Sofia flea market*

across the street. ⓐ Tsar Osvoboditel Blvd. 8A ⓣ (02) 981 8878
🕐 11.30–23.30

Mamma Mia £ ❷ Cheap and cheerful pasta and pizza restaurant with
upstairs tables on a terrace; the tables on your left as you enter the
courtyard belong to the cosy Mediterrani bar, which is under its own
management. ⓐ Tsar Shishman Street 39 ⓣ (02) 981 2727 🕐 10.00–00.00

Onda £ ❸ A very Western-style joint where latte-sipping café
habitués will feel at home. Cookies, muffins and sandwiches are
on the menu and, upstairs, more fine views of the Russian Church.
Wireless internet connection is available here. ⓐ Tsar Osvoboditel
Blvd. 8 ⓣ (02) 987 4920 🕐 07.00–21.00

AFTER DARK

RESTAURANTS

Victoria £ ❹ This is a fabulous restaurant with delicious thin crispy
pizzas, a great selection of pasta dishes, and luxuriant fresh salads.
Its back garden overlooking Alexander Nevsky Square is delightful
in summer. The menu also offers a wide range of wines. ⓐ Tsar
Osvoboditel Blvd. 7 ⓣ (02) 986 3200 🕐 24 hours

Bibliotekata ££ ❺ Nothing academic about this combined sushi bar,
set apart in a traditional Japanese setting, and adjoining live-music
club in the basement of the National Library. Over a dozen choices
of sushi and plenty of main dishes along the lines of scallop with
cream, spicy sauce, teriyaki chicken, beef teppanyaki and a dessert
of ice cream tempura! ⓐ Vasil Levski Blvd. 88 ⓣ (02) 943 4004
🕐 Sushi bar 12.00–01.30; Club 21.30–04.00

Egur, Egur ££ ❻ Armenian restaurant where the wallpaper, varnished wood flooring and (unplayed) piano create a homely and comfortable mood. Appetising starters like the Armenian sausages or *shtoratz* (fried aubergine rolls), followed by mostly meat-based dishes like *massis* (chicken stuffed with salmon and spinach) with a choice of tasty garnishes. 🅐 Dobrudzha Street 10 ☎ (02) 989 3383 🕐 11.30–00.00

Mahaloto ££ ❼ Mahaloto (Bulgarian for 'pendulum') is rather special because it creates an intimate restaurant atmosphere without sacrificing the need for carefully prepared meals and good service. There are familiar Bulgarian dishes on the menu but the more Western dishes are equally good – a rare achievement – and there is a decent wine list (though no cocktails). A brick cellar setting but tables also outside in the summer. 🅐 Vasil Levski Blvd. 51 ☎ 0887 617972 🕐 11.00–00.00

Checkpoint Charly £££ ❽ The name refers to the crossing point on the Berlin Wall, and the Cold War theme is playfully persistent in this stylish restaurant – the placemats reproduce Bulgaria's old Communist newspaper. At weekends a live jazz band performs. The food is international and receives good reviews. 🅐 Ivan Vazov Street 12 ☎ (02) 988 0370 🕐 10.00–00.00 Mon–Fri, 10.00 02.00 Sat & Sun

Krim £££ ❾ The most stately of Sofia's restaurants, set in and outside a 19th-century grand house, and one of the few that has survived from the Communist era. Bulgarian, Russian and fish dishes. 🅐 Slavyanska Street 17 ☎ (02) 988 6950 🕐 12.00–00.00

Uno Enoteca £££ ❿ One of Sofia's very best and most European restaurants. Come here for an atmosphere of subdued elegance.

Starters include Parma ham with melon, foie gras or a Caesar salad, and the choice of dishes will satisfy carnivores and vegetarians. An exemplary wine list and impeccable service. ⓐ Vasil Levski Blvd. 45 ⓣ (02) 981 4372 ⓦ www.uno-sofia.com ⓛ 12.00–00.00

NIGHTLIFE

Jack Piano Bar A basement bar beneath the Bulgarian Army Theatre where a grand piano is brought into play at night and music belted out until the early hours. Sociable and stylish and a great place to drop into after dinner. ⓐ Rakovski Street 98 ⓣ (02) 987 9198 ⓛ 20.00–04.00

My Mojito Dark and cosy club with two DJs spinning soft and soothing sounds in separate rooms – a relaxed watering hole for Sofia's sophisticated young ones; a good list of cocktails and a sociable atmosphere. ⓐ Ivan Vazov Street 14 ⓣ 0877 460400 ⓛ 21.00–05.00

Planet Club No matter whether you go for a cup of coffee, lunch or a drink in the evening you will always feel comfortable in this place, just gazing at the photos from movies and the various musical instruments hanging on the walls. Just behind the Alexander Nevsky Memorial Church. ⓐ Oborishte Street 1A ⓣ (02) 981 3532 ⓛ 09.00–04.00

Yalta Very close to Radisson SAS Grand Hotel, this is one of the hot spots in Sofia's club scene and regularly hosts famous international DJs. Stylish modern interior and plenty of beautiful young creatures. ⓐ Tsar Osvoboditel Blvd. 20 ⓣ (02) 987 3481 ⓛ 20.00–06.00

🔺 *The lively Jack Piano Bar*

Around Vitosha Boulevard

Vitosha Boulevard begins at the southern side of Sveta Nedelya Square and stretches south in a long straight line as if heading directly for Mount Vitosha (see page 116), which looms attractively in the distance. Once filled with traffic, Vitosha Boulevard is now barred to vehicles except for the clunking trams that trundle up and down, lending a pleasantly old-fashioned feel to the broad street. The mostly featureless buildings that line each side of the boulevard have been converted at street level into upmarket shops, and Vitosha Boulevard is now the premier shopping area for city residents; the all-too-familiar brand names and logos help to make it the most European-looking part of Sofia. The triumph of consumerism in this area leaves little space for cultural attractions, although the boulevard does lead to the National Palace of Culture (see page 94) and a large green area devoted to rest and relaxation.

SIGHTS & ATTRACTIONS

Earth and Man National Museum

Here you'll find literally thousands of exhibits of minerals, giant crystals and precious stones. The museum also hosts chamber concerts and all sorts of other cultural and charity events. ➌ Cherni Vrah Blvd. 4 ➊ (02) 865 6639 ➌ 10.00–18.00 Tues–Sat, closed Sun & Mon. Admission charge

Monument to the Bulgarian State

As you enter NDK Garden at the junction of Vitosha Boulevard and Patriarh Evtimii Boulevard, look for what resembles a grotesquely vandalised structure. This hideous metal agglomeration is the

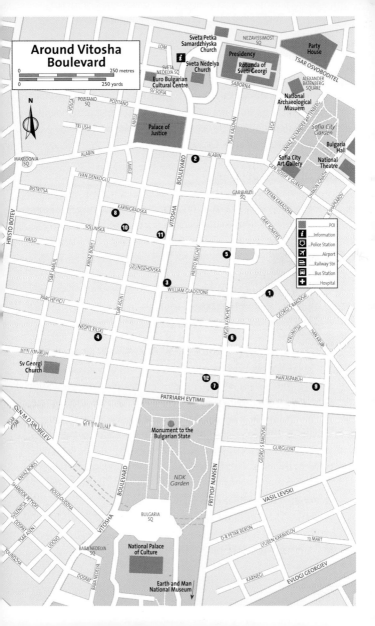

Around Vitosha Boulevard

0   250 metres

0   250 yards

N

Sveta Petka Samardzhiyska Church

Presidency

Rotunda of Sveti Georgi

Party House

TSAR OSVOBODITEL

NEZAVISSIMOST SQ

LOM

SVETA NEDELYA SQ

Sveta Nedelya Church

Euro Bulgarian Cultural Centre

SV SOFIA

SABORNA

TSAR KALOMAN

LECE

ALEXANDER BATENBERG SQUARE

National Archaeological Museum

KNIAZ ALEXANDER BATENBERG

Sofia City Garden

VOLGA

POZITANO SQ

POZITANO

TRI USHI

LAVELE

Palace of Justice

BOULEVARD

ALABIN

Sofia City Art Gallery

GEN YOSSIF V. GURO

Bulgaria Hall

National Theatre

V. CHAPKAROV

MAKEDONIA SQ

ALABIN

IVAN DENKOGLU

LAVELE

VITOSHA

GARIBALDI SQ

STEFAN KARADZHA

GRAOVITSA

DIAKON IGNATIY

BISTRITSA

KARNIGRADSKA

8

SOLUNSKA

10

11

HRISTO BOTEV

IVAILO

TSAR SAMUIL

KNIAZ BORIS I

UZUNDZHOVSKA

HRISTO BELCHEV

5

3

WILLIAM GLADSTONE

1

GEORGI S RAKOVSKI

STEUMISTE

HAN KRUB

PARCHEVICH

TSAR ASEN

NEOFIT RILSKI

4

ANGEL KANCHEV

6

HAN ASPARUH

Sv Georgi Church

12
7

MAIN ASPARUH

9

PATRIARH EVTIMII

GURGULYAT

GOLO BULDAR

Monument to the Bulgarian State

FRITYOF NANSEN

GEORGI S RAKOVSKI

GURGULYAT

GEN M D SKOBELEV

NDK Garden

VASIL LEVSKI

TSAR ISHAN

KNIAZ BORIS I

BOULEVARD

VITOSHA

DOSPAT ASEN

SHANDOR PETYOFI

SVILENITSA

TSAR ASEN

UJOVO

DOSPAT

VITOSHA

BABA NEDELYA

BABA NEDELYA SQ

DOSPAT

BULGARIA SQ

National Palace of Culture

D-R PETAR BERON

LYUBEN KARAVELOV

13 MART

KARNEGI

EVLOGI GEORGIEV

Earth and Man National Museum

POI
Information
Police Station
Airport
Railway Stn
Bus Station
Hospital

Monument to the Bulgarian State, built in 1981 to mark the thirteen hundred years anniversary of AD 681 when Han Asparuh led the Bulgars into what is now Bulgaria. What you see is a strong contender for the ugliest example of Soviet-era public art anywhere in the world.
❸ Northern end of NDK Garden

National Palace of Culture
Usually referred to as NDK, this monstrous edifice was constructed in 1981 to celebrate the country's 13th centenary, although it now seems only to celebrate the worst excesses of unimaginative

NDK GARDEN

This is the most popular park for the city's youth, and every evening and weekend the place is like a magnet for teenagers who hang out here with their skateboards or simply sit and dangle their legs over the concrete parapets – the pedestrian bridge that leads from behind the NDK towards the Hilton Hotel is a favourite spot for romantically inclined couples. There are kiosks selling candyfloss and drinks, and just before the pedestrian bridge a bar with outdoor aluminium seating where a drink and a snack can be enjoyed in the daytime or at night. It is only on the other side of the Hilton that actual greenery makes an appearance and even then it has a fairly unkempt look that tends to put you off wandering through it.
❸ Between Vitosha Blvd. and Frityof Nansen, beginning where Vitosha Blvd. meets Patriarh Evtimii Blvd.

▶ *The Monument to the Bulgarian State*

● *National Palace of Culture (NDK)*

architects who worked for the government in the Communist era. It houses concert halls, an exhibition space and shops. ● Bulgaria Sq. 1 ❶ Ticket office (02) 916 6369 ● 09.00–19.00

RETAIL THERAPY

Art Alley Gallery Bulgarian and international art for sale, based around exhibitions that tend to change every month or so, with any necessary packing arranged by the shop. (From Vitosha Boulevard,

turn into William Gladstone Street and cross two blocks; the shop is on your right just after crossing Angel Kanchev Street at the end of the second block.) ⊖ William Gladstone Street 51A ① (02) 986 7363 ⊕ 10.00–20.00 Tues–Sun, closed Mon

Bitsiani A fashion store with a reasonably large stock of snazzy jackets, shirts and ties. Shoes are on the level above and sportswear is downstairs. There is also a branch at Pirotska Street 18 and another one at Graf Ignatiev Street 23. ⊖ Vitosha Blvd. 32 ① (02) 989 7409 ⊕ 10.00–20.00 Mon–Sat, 11.00–19.00 Sun

THE CITY

▲ Sveta Sofia statue at the end of Vitosha Boulevard

98

Gallery Miniature To find this wonderful little gallery, walk down Vitosha Boulevard from Sveta Nedelya Church and take the fourth turning on the right, Karnigradska Street, and turn left off it after passing J.J. Murphy's pub. This brings you on to Kniaz Boris I Street and the gallery is down here on the right side. Nikola Litchkov is the sculptor and his son Milen the graphic artist, and between them they produce some excellent work. ⓐ Kniaz Boris I Street 55 ❶ (02) 986 5439 ❸ 10.00–18.00

Knigomania The best bookshop for English-language material, including hiking maps of Mount Vitosha. ⓐ Vitosha Blvd. 9 ❶ (02) 987 1859 ⓦ www.knigomania.bg ❸ 09.30–19.30 Mon–Fri, 10.00–18.00 Sat & Sun

Orange Multi-media store with four floors of stationery, toys, Bulgarian and foreign books and a broad selection of CDs, DVDs and games. There are copying and printing services in the basement and a nice restaurant on the fifth floor where you can stop for a cup of coffee. ⓐ Graf Ignatiev Street 18 ❶ (02) 981 0400 ❸ 09.00–21.00 Mon–Fri, 10.00–20.00 Sat & Sun

Pamela Megan This expensive boutique is at the bottom end of Vitosha Boulevard, just past the junction with Patriarh Evtimii Boulevard and the entrance to NDK Garden. Upmarket designs from Italy, France and Greece for fashion-conscious women. There are two other shops close by on the same stretch of street, Paola Apsi and Victor Uomo, under the same management and retailing similar gear. ⓐ Vitosha Blvd. 86 ❶ (02) 952 6812 ❸ 10.00–20.00 Mon–Fri, 10.30–19.30 Sat, closed Sun

TAKING A BREAK

Divaka £ ❶ Just near Slaveykov Square you can sample simple but hearty Bulgarian cuisine. The menu may not be extensive, but everything on it is tasty, fresh and inexpensive. ❷ William Gladstone Street 54 ❸ (02) 989 9543 ❹ 24 hours

Dream House £ ❷ Look for a sign for the entrance to the Internet Hostel, open the white door on the left and walk up the staircase to reach this vegetarian restaurant. Snack on starters like vegetable sushi in a spicy sauce with an avocado salad or make a meal of it with tofu and rice in sweet and sour sauce, or grilled courgette and tahini sauce. An eatery during the day but more restaurant-like at night; a buffet all day Sunday. Good drinks list. ❷ Alabin Street 50A ❸ (02) 980 8163 ❹ 11.30–22.00

Ugo £ ❸ Reasonable pizzas plus reasonable prices plus a great atmosphere equals very popular. ❷ Vitosha Boulevard 45 ❸ (02) 988 1892 ❹ 24 hours

Villa Rosiche £ ❹ Look for a blue plaque on the wall outside, and if you find yourself passing the Niky Hotel, you've missed it. Tucked away in a quiet courtyard, this is a neat little hideaway from the hubbub of Vitosha Boulevard. Cakes and chocolate truffles, coffees and a tempting choice of croissants, including ones stuffed with mozzarella and tomato or brie and broccoli. Cocktails and fruit drinks, with outdoor tables in the shade. ❷ Neofit Rilski Street 26 ❸ (02) 954 3072 ❹ 08.00–21.00

◯ *Enjoy sweet pastries at Villa Rosiche*

AFTER DARK

RESTAURANTS

Dani's £ ❺ Excellent little deli-café, ideal for a lunch break on a warm day when the home-made lemonade goes down a treat with a salad, soup and sandwich. ⓐ Angel Kanchev 18A ⓣ (02) 980 4548 ⓛ 10.00–22.00

Annette ££ ❻ Seated on couches and soft pillows, with exotic music and the warm light of hundreds of candles, one senses the vibe of a Moroccan night. Fab couscous and exotic salads. ⓐ Angel Kanchev Street 27 ⓣ (02) 980 4098 ⓦ www.annette.bg ⓛ 12.00–00.00

The Fox & Hound ££ ❼ Aha! A traditional pub atmosphere. The menu includes classical Bulgarian dishes as well as a wide range of European food. It's worth trying broccoli and blue cheese soup, or lamb meatballs with spinach, if you fancy a pub lunch with a difference. ⓐ Angel Kanchev Street 34 ⓣ (02) 980 7427 ⓛ 10.00–00.00

J.J. Murphy's ££ ❽ All too familiar Irish-themed pub in some respects, but reassuring when it comes to delivering a decent pint of Murphy's and recognisable dishes like shepherd's pie. This is also the best place to be sure of catching a satellite-transmitted football match. ⓐ Karnigradska Street 6 ⓣ (02) 980 2870 ⓛ 12.00–00.00

Manastirska Magernitsa ££ ❾ A contender for that last night in the city when you want a leisurely dining experience and a reminder that you are well and truly in the Balkans. The setting is perfect – a 19th-century house decorated in traditional Bulgarian style – for a menu of time-honoured dishes from the country's many monasteries. ⓐ Han Asparuh Street 67 ⓣ (02) 980 3883 ⓦ www.magernitsa.com ⓛ 11.00–02.00

Pri Yafata ££ ⑩ A good place to start satisfying your curiosity about Bulgarian cuisine because the grilled meats and salads are authentic national favourites. The décor looks kitschy but is actually genuine. ⓐ Solunska Street 28 ⓣ (02) 980 1727 ⓛ 10.00–01.00

Upstairs ££ ⑪ Fashionable diner with metal chairs on a narrow balcony overlooking Sofia's main drag, and tables and sofas in the arty interior. You can turn up for just drinks and enjoy the scene or tuck into the salads, pasta or dishes like chicken satay and pineapple. Coffees include a Drambuie-topped 'Prince Charles' ('for refined gentlemen') and plenty of cocktails. ⓐ Vitosha Blvd. 18 ⓣ (02) 989 9696 ⓛ 09.00–02.00 Mon–Fri, 10.00–02.00 Sat & Sun

Da Vidi £££ ⑫ The minimalist style and floor-to-ceiling windows may be a familiar format in other European cities, but this is hip stuff for Sofia and makes for an agreeable night out. The continental-style food is well-prepared with excellent fish dishes, and the wine list goes well beyond the national confines ⓐ Han Asparuh Street 36 ⓣ (02) 980 6746 ⓛ 11.00–22.00 Mon–Sat, 18.00–22.00 Sun

NIGHTLIFE

Escape Escape is Sofia's number-one nightclub, where techno and house music is belted out from the top notch sound system. High-flying DJs are part of the attraction. Sophisticated in many respects, and it rightly brags about Jean-Claude Van Damme turning up here one night. ⓐ Angel Kanchev Street 1 ⓣ 0889 990000 ⓛ 22.00–04.00 Thur–Sat, closed Sun–Wed

Life House A trendy club with stylish and modern design that whacks out house music. ⓐ Vitosha Blvd. 12 ⓣ 0888 241016 ⓛ 23.00–06.00. Admission charge

Outside the centre

Sofia's most significant cultural attractions, the medieval frescoes at Boyana Church and the National History Museum, are located 8 km (5 miles) southwest of the city centre in the affluent suburb of Boyana. It is a 20-minute ride by taxi and, although it takes over an hour by public transport, the bus journey is straightforward enough. Begin by catching tram No 9 on Makedonia Square, a five-minute walk away from Sveta Nedelya Square, to its terminus at Hladilnika. From here, it takes half a minute to walk through the tiny market of wooden stalls – just follow fellow passengers – to the street with a number of bus stops. Turn left and walk 300 m (330 yds) past the bus stops to an open area with more bus stops, and look for the one indicating bus No 64, which goes past Boyana Church. Bus No 63 from Toteben Boulevard passes the National History Museum, or catch trolleybus No 2 from outside Sofia University to its terminus and then walk up to and cross the main street, turn left and walk 200 m (219 yds) for an entrance road to the museum.

The other sights and attractions outside the centre are reachable on foot or by a short taxi ride.

SIGHTS & ATTRACTIONS

Borisova Gradina

From the Soviet Army Monument, it is a minute's walk to the entrance of the city's most spacious and attractive park and two stadiums. Renamed Borisova Gradina (Boris Garden) after 1989, it is still widely known as Freedom Park – a name associated with the Communist era and officially discarded for this reason. Developed and perfected by three successive gardeners, the park is large enough never to feel

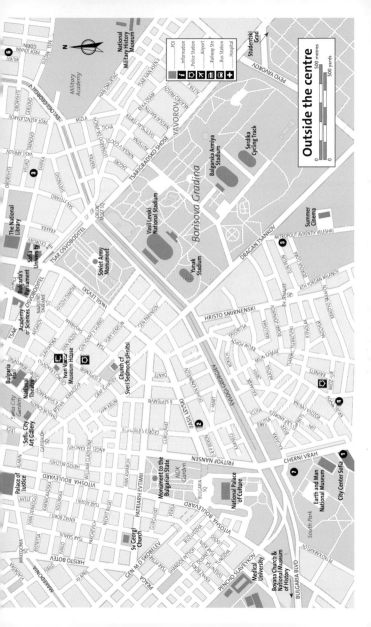

Outside the centre

0 ___ 500 metres
0 ___ 500 yards

POI
Information
Police Station
Airport
Railway Stn
Bus Station
Hospital

National Military History Museum

Military Academy

Borisova Gradina

Balgarska Armiya Stadium

Serdika Cycling Track

Vasil Levski National Stadium

Yunak Stadium

Summer Cinema

Soviet Army Monument

The National Library

Sofia University

Bulgaria's Parliament

Academy of Sciences

Bulgaria Hall

National Theatre

Ivan Vazov Museum House

Church of Sveti Sedmoch Slmitsi

Sofia City Garden

Sofia City Art Gallery

Palace of Justice

Monument to the Bulgarian State

NDK Garden

National Palace of Culture

South Park

Sv Georgi Church

Medical University

Boyana Church & National Museum of History

Earth and Man National Museum

City Center Sofia

Studentski Grad

HRISTO SMIRNENSKI

CHERNI VRAH

VITOSHA BOULEVARD

BULGARIA BLVD

PENCHO SLAVEYKOV

HRISTO BOTEV

GEN M D SKOBELEV

crowded, and joggers have the footpaths to themselves early in the morning. Ideal for picnics on a warm day. ➋ South of Orlov Most 🕒 24 hours

Soviet Army Monument

From Narodno Sabranie Square, Tsar Osvoboditel Boulevard heads towards Orlov Most (Eagles' Bridge), which crosses the puny River Perlovska. The bridge marks the spot where returning Bulgarian prisoners of war, released from Ottoman prisons after liberation in 1878, were greeted rapturously by their fellow citizens. The prisoners were christened 'the eagles', hence the creatures adorning the bridge on each side.

Before reaching the bridge, you will see the Soviet Army Monument, erected in 1954 to acknowledge the liberation of the country from Nazi submission (see page 14). These days, skateboarders hone their skills around the monument, seemingly oblivious to their own history. ➋ Tsar Osvoboditel Blvd. near Orlov Most

CULTURE

Boyana Church

The work of anonymous 13th-century artists, the church frescoes are Bulgaria's most important contribution to medieval European culture – not least because they are so well preserved and complete – and careful restoration work shows just how astonishing the artists' achievement was. Art historians compare their mastery of pictorial realism, use of the vernacular and mature awareness of colour to the achievement of Giotto (who was not even born when work began on these frescoes), founder of the Florentine school of painting and harbinger of the Italian Renaissance. How influential the Boyana

● *The Soviet Army Monument*

⬤ *Rear view of the ancient Boyana Church*

artists were in the development of Western European painting is the subject of debate, though there is no disputing their effect on mural painting in Russia and Eastern Europe. Although the frescoes pay homage to the canon of medieval icon painting and the traditions of Byzantine art, there is no mistaking the innovatory display of individuality and celebration of ordinary life in the more than 240 figures that populate the frescoes.

Visitor numbers and their time inside the church are strictly limited, and to study the frescoes in detail you will need to visit the nearby church museum where reproductions are on display. ⓐ Boyansko Ezero Street 1-3, Boyana ⓣ (02) 959 0939 ⓦ www.boyanachurch.org ⓛ 09.30–17.30. Admission charge

National History Museum

The city and the country's most prestigious museum, once located in the heart of the city, was moved to the suburb of Boyana to make use of a grand palatial building once used by the Communist government. What you will see here is an engaging ethnographic exhibition on the top floor, assorted artefacts from the ancient times and the Middle Ages, and a collection of frescoes from monasteries around the country. ⓐ Vitoshko Lale 16, Boyana ⓣ (02) 955 4280 ⓦ www.historymuseum.org ⓛ 09.30–18.00 (Apr–Oct); 09.00–17.30 (Nov–Mar), closed on public holidays. Admission charge and additional charge for use of a camera

National Military History Museum

The paraphernalia in the cabinets inside the museum – uniforms, weapons and the like – will tend to appeal only to military buffs, but the hardware on show outside is the real draw. There are MiG jet fighters, missile launchers and SS23 missiles from the Soviet era

> **PATRON OF THE ARTS**
>
> In 1259, Sevastocrator Kaloyan expanded the church at Boyana
> and commissioned a group of artists – their names lost to
> posterity – to illuminate the interior with frescoes. One of
> the finest paintings you will see in Boyana depicts Kaloyan
> in the contemporary dress of nobles holding a model of the
> church in his hands alongside his wife, Desislava.

alongside the phenomenally versatile Russian T34 tank that played
a crucial role in the defeat of German forces by the USSR. ⓐ Cherkovna
Street 92 ⓣ (02) 946 1805 ⓛ. 10.00–18.00 Wed–Sun, closed Mon
& Tues. Admission charge

RETAIL THERAPY

City Center Sofia Huge complex with over 100 shops such as Marks
& Spencer, Guy Laroche, Calvin Klein, Bata and Nike. There's also
a buzzing fast-food area, several cafés and a Cineplex, with six cinema
halls. ⓐ Arsenalski Blvd. 2 ⓣ (02) 865 7285 ⓦ www.ccs-mall.com
ⓛ 10.00–22.00 ⓝ Tram: 6, 9

Traditzia A worthy, EU-funded project supporting ethnic minorities
and people with disabilities in Bulgaria by selling their handicrafts:
ceramics, hand-made stationery, glassware, kilims and linen.
The shop is on the south side of Vasil Levski Boulevard, close
to the junction with 6 September Street. ⓐ Vasil Levski Blvd. 36
ⓣ (02) 981 7765 ⓦ www.traditzia.bg ⓛ 11.00–19.00 Tues–Sat,
closed Sun & Mon

TAKING A BREAK

There is a small café inside the National History Museum (see page 109), but nothing in the immediate vicinity of Boyana Church, and so it is advisable to either bring picnic food or time your visit between meal times.

Fancy £ ❶ With its lively atmosphere, friendly and informal service and great variety of European food, this is the perfect place for a break in your shopping tour. ❸ Arsenalski Blvd. 2, City Center Sofia
❶ (02) 963 4480 ❶ 10.00–00.00

Fix Mix £ ❷ Big on cocktails, with at least 40 available, alongside salmon sandwiches and other tasty snacks. It's decorated in fruity colours, with light, modern furniture and funky music. ❸ Vasil Levski

⬤ *Pretty handicrafts make perfect souvenirs*

THE CITY

Blvd. 24 ☎ (02) 987 3171 ⓦ www.fixmix-culture.com ⏰ 08.00–22.00
Mon–Fri, 10.00–22.00 Sat & Sun

O! Shipka £ ❸ Well worth seeking out for an inexpensive but tasty
pizza, salad or Mexican-style dish. Tables inside, where sociability
raises the noise level, or a pleasant garden setting, where peace and
quiet can be enjoyed and a glass of wine or two sipped contentedly.
ⓐ Shipka Street 11 ☎ (02) 944 9288 ⏰ 24 hours

AFTER DARK

RESTAURANTS

Arkadia ££ ❹ Hidden away down a quiet street – walking down
Sveti Naum from the Hilton end, take the second left, but if you
reach the Lotenetz Hotel you have gone past the turning – this
restaurant and bar is not known to many visitors and it makes for
a perfect getaway and a quiet meal. The menu features a variety
of starters, more than half a dozen vegetarian dishes, fondue
(Bulgarian style) and all sorts of meats. Eat inside, downstairs

> ### STUDENTSKI GRAD
> Studentski Grad, 'student city', is a suburb 7 km (4 1/3 miles)
> southeast of the city centre and home to 10,000 bright young
> people intent on having a good time when not inside a lecture
> theatre. There are countless bars and pubs, and the neighbourhood
> can be reached by taking a bus from Shipka Street to the end
> of the line. You will need a taxi to get back to town but they
> are easy to find around the bars. ⓦ Bus: 94, 280

(where there is a snooker table and dartboard) or outside. A good list of Bulgarian wines. ⓐ Krum Popov Street 64 ⓣ (02) 865 8484 ⓛ 11.00–00.00

Pod Lipite ££ ❺ At the southwest side of Borisova Gradina, this restaurant is a must. Decorated in traditional Bulgarian style and featuring live folk music in the evenings, this is the perfect place to taste genuine meals prepared from old Bulgarian recipes. ⓐ Elin Pelin Street 5 ⓣ (02) 866 5053 ⓛ 12.00–01.00

Pri Miro ££ ❻ Either a fairly long walk from the centre of town or a short taxi ride is justified in order to experience this authentic Serbian restaurant. Bulgarians and Serbs share a love of grilled meats, and this is the place to taste the differences in style and taste. The firm favourites are the *pleskavice* (sausage-like patties of minced meat) and *cevapcici* (rissoles), and there are some very tasty relishes to go with either. One of Sofia's best restaurants. ⓐ Murfi Street 34 ⓣ (02) 943 7127 ⓦ www.restaurantmiro.com ⓛ 12.00–00.00

Seasons £££ ❼ Seasons has the best themed buffets in the city and Mondays, devoted to Bulgarian cuisine, provide an excellent introduction to the country's food. There is also an à la carte menu and, in the summer, tables on the terrace with views of Mount Vitosha. ⓐ Hilton Hotel, Bulgaria Blvd. 1 ⓣ (02) 933 5062 ⓛ 06.30–23.30

NIGHTLIFE
Bar Na Kraia Na Vselenata In English, this is named the 'Bar at the End of the Universe' and describes itself as themed around 'the fragmented remains of an eventually ruined planet, which is enclosed in a vast time bubble and projected forward in time

to the precise moment of The End of The Universe'. Very Douglas Adams! What you actually get is a large circular bar and brightly painted walls, plus a lively scene with a friendly atmosphere and a long list of cocktails. ⓐ Studentski Grad, Block 34, next to Entrance B ⓣ (02) 962 5541 ⓦ www.vselenata.com ⓛ 09.00–02.00

Marseille A café-club with a good reputation for party nights, especially at weekends, playing retro, latino, pop and rock. ⓐ Prof. Dr Ivan Stranski Street 5, Studentski Grad, between Blocks 55 and 56 ⓣ (02) 968 1977 ⓦ www.sakar-marsilia.com ⓛ 08.00–02.00

Swingin' Hall The best place in Sofia for everyone who likes live rock, pop and jazz performances, and it has two stages for alternating bands. ⓐ Dragan Tsankov Blvd. 8 ⓣ (02) 963 0696 ⓛ 21.00-04.00 Tues–Sun, closed Mon

Toucan Bluzz & Rock A pub that serves up live rock and blues. It also does the best karaoke in Sofia every Thursday night. ⓐ Akademik Boris Stefanov Street 4, Studentski Grad ⓣ 0887 098164 ⓛ 21.00–04.00

ⓞ *The stunningly beautiful Rila Monastery*

OUT OF TOWN

Mount Vitosha

Mount Vitosha is clearly visible from the city centre, and it only takes a 7-km (4 1/3-mile) bus ride to reach the foothills of this 2,290-m high (7,513-ft) outcrop of rock and pine forests. There are a number of marked trails through the woods and, outside winter, a day out with a picnic suggests itself as an ideal excursion from the city. You can take a bus to either Dragalevtsi and walk to a chairlift to Aleko from the village square, or to Simeonovo for a cable car to Aleko. A bus also goes directly to Aleko, and this would be your route if planning a skiing trip in winter.

GETTING THERE

By road
Hladilnika bus station, the one used to reach Boyana (see page 104), serves the Mount Vitosha area, and to reach the station take tram No 9 on Alabin Street a five-minute walk away from Sveta Nedelya Square. The tram terminates at Hladilnika, and, after getting off the tram, walk for half a minute through the small market of wooden stalls beside the tram lines. This brings you out onto a main street where you turn left and walk past a number of bus stops to a large open area where buses turn and where there is a ticket kiosk on your left and more bus stops. From here, bus No 64 goes to Dragalevtsi and Boyana villages; No 93 goes through the village and on to the chairlift; No 98 goes to Dragalevtsi and onto Simeonovo village; and No 122 goes to the Simeonovo cable car. You can use your usual tram tickets on these routes.

Bus No 66 goes to Aleko, but for this route you need to purchase a separate return ticket from the kiosk. The times of the return buses

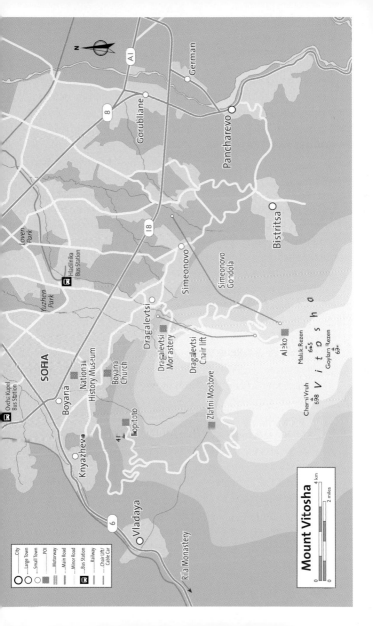

Mount Vitosha

Legend:
- ○ City
- ⊙ Large Town
- ○ Small Town
- ■ POI
- ⋯ Motorway
- — Main Road
- ⋯ Minor Road
- — Railway
- Ⓡ Bus Station
- ⋯ Chair Lift / Cable Car

SOFA

Ovtcи Kupel Bus Station

Knyazhevo

Boyana

National History Museum

Boyana Church

Zopitoto

41

Vladaya

Rila Monastery

Hladilnika Bus Station

Yuzhen Park

Loven Park

Dragalevtsi

Dragalevtsi Monastery

Dragalevtsi Chair lift

Zlatni Mostove

Simeonovo

Simeonovo Gondola

Gorubliane

German

Pancharevo

Bistritsa

Aleko

Malik Rezen 645

Goylam Rezen 691

V i t o s h a

Cherni Vruh 698

A1

8

18

6

0 — 4 km

0 — 2 miles

are posted on the window of the kiosk and it is worth taking note of these. There are eight a day; the first departure at 07.50 and the last return bus at 18.00.

SIGHTS & ATTRACTIONS

Aleko
Aleko styles itself as a winter resort, and it is the base for skiing but, skiing apart, the visitor infrastructure is decrepit and the sight of a disused hotel sinking into the snow is hardly inspiring. There is a functioning hotel with a restaurant at the point where the bus from Sofia terminates, and that is about it. From the hotel, it is a five-minute walk to the ski slopes. In summer, it takes less than an hour for an invigorating walk up to Cherni Vruh (Black Peak), the summit of Mount Vitosha.

Dragalevtsi
If you want to get off the bus at Dragalevtsi village, look for a lemon-painted building on the left side of the street and the cobbled Tsar Ivan Alexander Square. The journey from Hladilnika bus station only

---

SKIING ON MOUNT VITOSHA
Skiing lasts from late December through to early April, although the start and end times tend to vary from one year to the next. Aleko is the base, and this is where **Ski & Snowboard School Aleko Moten** (❶ (02) 967 1141 ❷ www.motensport.eu) is based. Skiing gear can be hired by the day. English-speaking instructors can be hired, subject to 24 hours' notice.

⬥ *Snow-capped Mount Vitosha*

takes about seven minutes. There are hotels with restaurants
in Dragalevtsi, and from here it takes about 40 minutes to walk
up to the chairlift. Facing the square from the bus stop, take the
road that begins in the top right corner of the square and, after
about half an hour, turn left off the road where a sign points to
the Vodenitzata restaurant. The chairlift is less than ten minutes
away up this road, and it stops at a mid-way station on its way
up to Aleko. ☎ Chairlift (02) 967 1125 🕐 08.30–16.30 Thur–Sun,
closed Mon–Wed

Simeonovo

The village of Simeonovo is less attractive than Dragalevtsi (which
itself is not especially eye-catching) and, with fewer amenities by
way of places to eat, the only reason to come here would be to take
the cable car up to Aleko. ☎ Cable car (02) 961 2189 🕐 08.30–18.00
Tues–Sun, closed Mon

Zlatni Mostove

Zlatni Mostove (Golden Bridges) is an attractive area of evergreen
forest and the misleadingly named Stone River, which is not really
a river but a dramatic series of huge boulders deposited at the
end of the last ice age under which flows a paltry stream. From
where the Sofia bus stops, there are a number of marked hiking
routes and, if you are making a day of it, take the one to Cherni
Vruh, the peak of Mount Vitosha. It takes almost three hours, so
be sure to bring water and food because there are no restaurants
along the way. What you do get is a mildly spectacular landscape
of peat bog. 🚍 Bus: 61 from Ovcha Kupel bus station in Sofia.
You will need to purchase a separate ticket for this route at the
bus station.

△ *The Stone River at Zlatni Mostove*

TAKING A BREAK

Helis Bar & Diner £ One of the coolest places in Dragalevtsi, with simple but perfect meals, a big TV screen and very friendly staff who create a homely and informal atmosphere. In the summer you can enjoy the panoramic view over Sofia. ⓐ Nartsis Street 6, Dragalevtsi ⓣ (0895) 708 010 ⓛ 09.00–23.30

Lyutite Chushki £–££ The menu features a full range of salads and other cold dishes like smoked salmon or shrimp cocktail, and many lunchtime meals such as chicken bites with bacon, aubergine pastry and meat rolls. Pork, chicken and fish meals are also available. To find the restaurant, keep the village square on your left and walk 200 m (219 yds) further along Krairechna Street, the road where the bus from Sofia stops, and it is on your right. ⓐ Krairechna Street 26, Dragalevtsi ⓣ (02) 967 2220 ⓦ www.lutitechushki.com ⓛ 11.00–01.00

The Old House £–££ One of the most pleasant places to enjoy a meal in Dragalevtsi, and you will find it by taking the road that leads from the village square to the chairlift. It is on the left, less than five minutes from the village and, although the name is not in English, is easy to identify by its rustic-looking, alpine exterior. ⓐ General Kovatchev Street 9, Dragalevtsi ⓣ (02) 967 3137 ⓛ 12.00–00.00

AFTER DARK

Hotel Darling Restaurant ££ Black caviar for starters, specialities such as fried trout and a host of chicken, veal and pork dishes help to make this restaurant well worth considering for an evening meal. ⓐ Yabalkova Gradina Street 14, Dragalevtsi ⓣ (02) 967 5018

Vodenitzata ££–£££ A folksy-looking, stone-built restaurant with an attractive garden area. The food is traditional Bulgarian, and evenings are enlivened by troupes of dancers in folk costumes. It is best to make a reservation at weekends because large groups can take over the place. ❸ By the Dragalevtsi chairlift, Dragalevtsi ❶ (02) 967 1058 ❺ 12.00–00.00

ACCOMMODATION

Darling £ The second-best hotel in Dragalevtsi, with room rates a little less than those of the Alexander Palace but with a better restaurant (see opposite). ❸ Yabalkova Gradina Street 14, Dragalevtsi ❶ (02) 967 5018 ❿ www.hotel-darling.com

Edi £ There are 14 inexpensive double rooms in this small but basically comfortable hotel, and a restaurant on the first floor as well as outdoor tables for food and drink. The Lyutite Chushki restaurant (see opposite) is next door. ❸ Krairechna Street 28, Dragalevtsi ❶ (02) 967 2270 ❶ (02) 967 2218 ❿ www.hoteledi.hit.bg

Alexander Palace ££ Close to the village square, this is the best hotel in Dragalevtsi in terms of amenities and general comfort. Standard rooms have a fridge and there is little to be gained by paying extra for one of the deluxe doubles. There is a restaurant and sauna. ❸ Nartsis Street 1, Dragalevtsi ❶ (02) 967 1184 ❶ (02) 967 3146 ❿ www.svetasofia-alexanders.com

Blagoevgrad

Two hours away by a regular bus service and 100 km (62 miles) south of Sofia, the university town of Blagoevgrad offers a day out to an animated and sophisticated city filled with bars, restaurants and a modicum of cultural attractions.

GETTING THERE

By road

Buses leave from Sofia's Central Bus Station (see page 53), up to ten a day and with most leaving in the morning, and stop either in front of Blagoevgrad's railway station or at the bus terminal, 200 m (219 yds) further along the road. If you are dropped off at the bus terminal, walk out on to the street, turn left and walk the 200 m (219 yds) to the railway station and the junction. Turn right at the junction and walk up Bratya Miladinovi, past the Alen Mak Hotel to the main – and clearly identified – American University of Bulgaria. If you go to the right in front of the main building and cut through the small park, this will bring you into town and straight to the pavement tables outside the Pizza Napoli restaurant. The centre of town is mostly pedestrianised, and the old part of town, Varosha, is on the other side of the small river and only a short walk away.

SIGHTS & ATTRACTIONS

Varosha

Varosha is the old quarter of the city, easy to reach on the other side of the river and readily identified by the cobbled streets and the traditional buildings that date back to the 19th century. Here

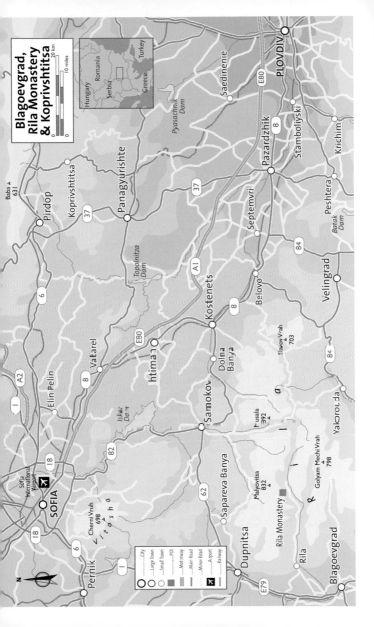

⬤ *Colourful detail from the church façade in Varosha*

you will find the Church of the Annunciation of the Virgin, its exterior characterised by red and white stripes and murals decorating the portico. The folksy-looking Kristo Hotel is directly above the church.

CULTURE

History Museum

A motley collection of assorted finds from ancient times, religious artefacts in the form of icons and carvings, and outbursts of colour in a fine display of traditional costumes from the region. There is also a natural history section made up of stuffed birds and animals. None of the labelling is in English, but the cost of admission includes a brochure in English. ⓐ Rila Street 1 ⓘ (073) 885 365 ⓛ 09.00–12.00, 13.00–18.00 Mon–Sat, closed Sun. Admission charge

RETAIL THERAPY

Mason Fairly typical of the small boutiques catering to the city's students and young people – cotton fabrics, funky, loose-fitting garments for both sexes – Mason is on the same street

RETAIL TRAUMA

For a shock-inducing glimpse of what shopping used to be like in the Soviet era, drop into the GUM department store. Its dark and gloomy interior, filled with displays so depressing that they act like an instant antidote to any consumerist urges, is left over from another age. ⓐ Directly opposite the Kristal café in Macedonia Square

as Tuborg (see below). **ⓐ** Bratya Kitanovi 10, Blagoevgrad
🕐 11.00–19.30

TAKING A BREAK

Kristal £ Always busy, with its outside tables dominating one corner of Macedonia Square, this is the place to sink into if you have an hour to spare to watch the world, well, Blagoevgrad, go by. **ⓐ** Macedonia Square, Blagoevgrad **🕐** 08.30–00.00

Tuborg £ A spacious and comfortable pub-restaurant on one of the pedestrianised streets running off Macedonia Square. Salads, spaghetti and meat dishes, with tables outside. **ⓐ** Bratya Kitanovi 25, Blagoevgrad **🕐** 08.00–01.00

Varosha Restaurant £ Situated between the museum and the church in the old part of town, this timbered two-storey building blends in perfectly with the traditional ambience of the neighbourhood. The menu is unexciting but adequate for a lunch break, and there are two tables on a neat little balcony overlooking the river and park where you could happily while away the time with a drink. **ⓐ** Bistritsa Street 10, Blagoevgrad **ⓣ** (073) 880 000 **🕐** 09.00–23.00

AFTER DARK

RESTAURANTS

Kristo £–££ On the first floor of the hotel and decked out in the traditional style that one would expect, this roomy restaurant has a menu that includes 40 different salads, hot and cold starters and grills. The dark wood décor gives the restaurant a rather sober atmosphere, and the best tables are those overlooking the cobbled courtyard. ⓐ Kristo Hotel, Komitrov Street, Varosha, Blagoevgrad ① (073) 880 444 ⓛ 10.00–00.00

Dreams ££ Around the corner from Pizza Napoli and upstairs from the Underground pub, this is the most formal restaurant in the city in the evening. The menu is not in English but staff should be able to translate; stick with the fish dishes because they're what they do best. ⓐ Arseni Kostentsev Street 7, Blagoevgrad ① (073) 834 526 ⓛ 09.00–01.00

NIGHTLIFE

Underground This is the most popular nightspot in Blagoevgrad, and the place is packed with students for the weekend discos. There is also a separate bar but it is hard to escape the sound system blasting out rock and pop-folk. ⓐ Arseni Kostentsev Street 7, Blagoevgrad ① (0899) 942211 ⓛ 20.00–02.00

Vertigo No food but a long drinks list and lots of cocktails. ⓐ Todor Alexandrov Street 3, Blagoevgrad ① (0899) 786322 ⓛ 24 hours

ACCOMMODATION

Kristo £ This would be the first choice for any overnight stay in Blagoevgrad. It is situated in the peaceful Varosha district but within walking distance of the city's nightlife. There are over 30 rooms with air-conditioning, a restaurant and bar (see opposite), and a sauna. ⓐ Komitrov Street, Varosha, Blagoevgrad ① (073) 880 444 ① (073) 880 555 ⓦ www.hotelkristo.net

Rila Monastery

The Rila Mountains lie to the south of Mount Vitosha, but it takes longer to reach the famed Rila Monastery, 120 km (75 miles) from Sofia. Although a day trip from the capital is feasible, most visitors spend a night outside Sofia in order to make the journey a less hectic one.

GETTING THERE

By road

The Ovcha Kupel bus station ((02) 955 5362), on Ovcha Kupel Boulevard, which is off Tsar Boris III Boulevard and southwest of the city centre, serves Rila Monastery. To reach the bus station, take tram No 5 from Alabin Street and, after about ten stops, you will see it on the right side of the street. Confirm the time of the first bus running direct to the monastery, and the last buses back, and catch the first bus if making a day trip from Sofia. A more leisurely itinerary would be to catch one of the numerous daily buses from Ovcha Kupel to Dupnitsa, and from there catch a local bus to the monastery, spending a night close to the monastery at Rilets Hotel or in the monastery itself.

SIGHTS & ATTRACTIONS

Rila Mountains

Quite apart from the attractions of the monastery itself, hiking the rural trails through the surrounding forests is reason enough to make an excursion to this famous valley in the Rila Mountains. A number of trails start from near the monastery and the shortest, less than an hour's walk, leads to St John of Rila's cave. This route begins 2 km (1 1/4 miles) east of the monastery's eastern gate (the main entrance

◆ *Emerald lakes in the Rila Mountains*

to the monastery is through the western gate) by taking the trail that heads left just after the Bachkova Cheshma restaurant. When you reach the cave, you can walk through it and come out the other side but it is unlit and very claustrophobic.

The main trails through the Rila Mountains are set out on a noticeboard in the monastery's car park, and a bracing walk can be enjoyed by taking any one of them. **a** Rila Monastery is 27 km (16 3/4 miles) east of Rila village on a signposted road that branches off the E79, 20 km (12 1/2 miles) south of Dupnitsa

CULTURE

Rila Monastery
Coming from Sofia, you arrive outside the fortress-like western gate and pass through it into a serene courtyard surrounded by stylish striped arcades, tiers of monastic chambers and graceful balconies.

THE HISTORY OF THE MONASTERY
The monastery owes its origins to Ivan Rilski, now known as St John of Rila, a 9th-century hermit monk who acquired a band of devotees after lengthy sojourns in the wild, and eventually founded a hermitage in the Rila Mountains. The first monastery, a short distance from the original hermitage, was founded in 1335 and became a major spiritual centre during the Middle Ages. It survived for half a millennium until it was accidentally burned down in the 19th century; rebuilding started within a year and what you see today was added to UNESCO's list of World Heritage Sites in the early 1980s.

Climb the staircase to the top balcony to take in the scenery. The monastery's kitchen, in the west wing to the left of the church that occupies the centre of the courtyard, is well worth a visit.

The church museum is to be found in the east wing. Its claim to fame is a late 18th-century wooden cross, intricately inscribed with 140 biblical scenes and 1,500 human figures, the work of one monk who devoted 12 years of his life to the task and lost his eyesight as a consequence of spending hours squinting through a magnifying glass. ② Rila Monastery, 27 km (16 3/4 miles) east of Rila village, off the E79, 20 km (12 1/2 miles) south of Dupnitsa ① 06.00–22.00 (summer); 08.00–18.00 (winter); Museum: 08.00–17.00. Admission charge for museum (but not to monastery)

Rila Monastery Church

Built in the 1830s and the largest monastery church in the country, the exterior is covered in murals and the interior walls are adorned with frescoes, all of which invite close scrutiny for their pictorial spectacles and wealth of detail. ① 06.00–22.00 (summer); 08.00–18.00 (winter)

TAKING A BREAK

Rila Monastery Bakery £ A monkish repast of *mekitsi* (deep-fried doughnuts), bread and sheep yogurt. ② Outside the east gate of Rila Monastery ① 06.00–22.00 (summer); 08.00–18.00 (winter)

Restaurant Drushlyavitsa £–££ This is easily the most attractive place for a meal when visiting Rila Monastery: a scenic location with outdoor tables taking advantage of the views and a full menu of Bulgarian dishes and fresh trout. ② Outside the east gate of Rila Monastery ① 08.00–22.00

ACCOMMODATION

Rila Monastery £ Spartan accommodation in monks' cells is available at the monastery but you will have to do without hot water. Check what time the monastery gates close and plan accordingly for dinner. ⓐ Rila Monastery ⓣ (0896) 872010

Rilets £ A 15-minute walk from the eastern gate of Rila Monastery brings you to this featureless but functional hotel. It would do for a one-night stopover and there is a restaurant, although it would be better to eat at Restaurant Drushlyavitsa (see page 133) and get back to the hotel before dark. ⓐ Rila Monastery area ⓣ (07054) 2106

You can stay overnight at Rila Monastery

Koprivshtitsa

This small town, 75 km (46 1/2 miles) east of Sofia, played a key role in an insurrection against Ottoman rule in 1876 called the April Uprising. It takes about two hours to reach Koprivshtitsa from Sofia by public transport, using one of the two minibuses that depart daily in the morning from the Trafik-Market bus terminal next to the Central Railway Station (see page 52). The bus stop in Koprivshtitsa is in the middle of town and it is a short walk northwards, following the river, to reach the main 20 April Square. In the northwest corner of the square, at No 6, there is a tourist information centre (❶ (07184) 2191 🕐 erratic, but officially 09.00–18.00). Two doors up is the Kupchiinitsa (museums' office 🕐 09.00–17.00), and here you can purchase a combined ticket for the town's six museum houses; this saves money if you visit more than two of them but otherwise pay individually at each museum. Try to avoid visiting the town on Monday and Tuesday, when many of the house museums are closed. The best museum house to see from the outside is Oslekov House; the best interior is Lyutov House.

SIGHTS & ATTRACTIONS

Oslekov House

This house was built in the middle of the 19th century for a rich merchant family, and the façade is painted with cityscapes of Rome, Venice and Padua – places visited by the merchant. A timber staircase leads to a hall, and a set of rooms laid out with exhibits relating to the history of the house and the lifestyle of its inhabitants. The house

❶ *Mother of local poet Dimcho Debelyanov waits for him to return from WWI*

is a couple of minutes away on foot and uphill from 20 April Square.
ⓐ Hadzhi Nencho Palaveev Blvd. 39 ⓣ (01784) 2555 ⓛ 09.30–17.00
Tues–Sun, closed Mon. Admission charge

Dimcho Debelyanov House

From Oslekov House, continue uphill and turn the corner into
Dimcho Debelyanov Street to find this house on the left-hand side
after 100 m (110 yds). Birthplace of the poet Dimcho Debelyanov
(1887–1916), the exhibits on display relate to his tragic life but the
captions are woefully inadequate. Debelyanov was killed in World
War I, and his love life was marred by the early death of a woman
whose father killed her to prevent her relationship with Debelyanov
continuing. ⓐ Dimcho Debelyanov Street 6 ⓣ (01784) 2077
ⓛ 09.30–17.00 Tues–Sun, closed Mon. Admission charge

Todor Kableshkov House

From Dimcho Debelyanov House, return and turn right to reach
the top of the hill and the town cemetery. Over the grave of the
poet stands a statue, and the small church is also worth a visit.
If you turn left after leaving the churchyard on the side opposite
to where you came in, you will find Todor Kableshkov House some
40 m (44 yds) down the street on your left. The interior is devoted
to displays of material relating to the April Uprising, the house
being the birthplace of the hero who began the insurrection.
ⓐ Todor Kableshkov Street 8 ⓣ (01784) 2054 ⓛ 09.30–17.00
Tues–Sun, closed Mon. Admission charge

Lyutov House

Cross the bridge after leaving Todor Kableshkov Street and turn left
into Nikola Belovezhdov Street to find the white-painted Lyutov House

⬥ *Overlooking the town*

on your left after 100 m (110 yds). The home of a rich and much-travelled merchant, the interior is richly decorated with murals of European locations visited by the merchant, ornately carved ceilings and Viennese furniture. ⓐ Nikola Belovezhdov Street 2 ⓣ (01784) 2138 ⓛ 09.30–17.00 Wed–Mon, closed Tues. Admission charge

TAKING A BREAK

Bulgaria £ This restaurant has a lovely terrace as well as tables in a comfortable dining area that evokes times past. It is situated on the main street that runs by the side of the river and links the bus stop with 20 April Square, but at its northern end and beyond the main square. ⓐ Hadzhi Nencho Palaveev Blvd. 31 ⓣ (01784) 2183 ⓛ 09.00–22.30

Chuchura £ Easy to find, close by the bus stop, this inexpensive eatery is very convenient if you arrive in town feeling hungry and thirsty after the journey from Sofia. Do not be put off by the unprepossessing exterior: the food is good and relies on traditional Bulgarian favourites. ⓐ Hadzhi Nencho Palaveev Blvd. 66 ⓣ (01784) 2712 ⓛ 09.00–22.30

Pod Starata Krusha £ This pub-restaurant is cheap and cheerful and offers a good range of drinks and meals throughout the day and evening. ⓐ Hadzhi Nencho Palaveev Blvd. 56 ⓣ (01784) 2163 ⓛ 08.30–22.30

AFTER DARK

RESTAURANT
Dyado Liben £ This restaurant, on the eastern side of the river and reached by a bridge from the town square, is set in a picturesque old house with an attractive cobbled courtyard and inside seating upstairs. The food is not particularly different to what is found on other restaurant menus in Koprivshtitsa, but the old building and furnishings lend an atmosphere ideally suited for an evening out. ⓐ Hadzhi Nencho Palaveev Blvd. 47 ⓣ (01784) 2109 ⓛ 09.00–22.00

⬟ *Typical Renaissance house in Koprivshtitsa*

ACCOMMODATION

Accommodation can be booked at the tourist information office but there should be no problem finding a place to stay. Hotels, usually small family-run affairs, are dotted around town and room rates are fairly uniform and very affordable.

Astra £ At the northeast corner of the village, 0.5 km (half a mile) from the town square and on the other side of the river, this family-run guesthouse has comfortable rooms in a traditional setting and benefits from a pretty courtyard where you can sit with a beer or two and see the evening out. ⓐ Hadzhi Nencho Palaveev Blvd. 11 ⓣ (01784) 2033 ⓦ www.hotelastra.org

Bashtina Kushta £ If you want a break from the folksy style that characterises most places in town, this modern hostelry fits the bill. Uncomplicated rooms and attic ones with sloping ceilings. Walk north from the town square and it is on your left after 150 m (164 yds). ⓐ Hadzhi Nencho Palaveev Blvd. 32 ⓣ (01784) 3033 ⓦ www.fhhotel.info

🔘 *Sofia is a short flight away from the UK*

PRACTICAL
information

Directory

GETTING THERE

By air

British Airways and Bulgaria Air fly direct from London (3 hours and 20 minutes) but their fares are expensive. Wizzair flies direct from Luton with reasonable fares as well as easyJet from Gatwick. Indirect fares via other European cities, and with other airlines, offer the best fare deals. Malev Hungarian Airlines, for example, flies to Sofia via Budapest from the UK and Ireland. Also, check out specialist agents like Balkan Holidays and compare their prices.

Balkan Holidays ☎ 0845 130 1114 🌐 www.balkanholidays.co.uk
British Airways ☎ 0845 773 3377 🌐 www.britishairways.com
Bulgaria Air ☎ 020 7637 7637 🌐 www.bulgaria-air.co.uk
easyJet 🌐 www.easyjet.com
Malev ☎ 020 7439 0577 🌐 www.malev.hu
Regent Holidays ☎ 0117 921 1711 🌐 www.regent-holidays.co.uk
Wizzair 🌐 www.wizzair.com

Travellers from North America, Australia and New Zealand should fly first to a major European air transport hub, and from there to Sofia.

Many people are aware that air travel emits CO_2, which contributes to climate change. You may be interested in the possibility of lessening the environmental impact of your flight through the charity Climate Care, which offsets your CO_2 by funding environmental projects around the world. Visit 🌐 www.climatecare.org

By rail

There are various rail routes but, at the moment, it is still not possible to buy a through train ticket to Sofia. The closest you can get is a booked ticket to Budapest and, once there, no problem should arise booking a ticket for the daily Budapest–Sofia train service. It will take about 24 hours to reach Budapest from London (Eurostar to Paris and on from there by sleeper via Vienna or Munich), and the last leg of the journey, Budapest–Sofia, will take that long again. Some informative sites to check out are:

The Man in Seat 61 Ⓦ www.seat61.com

Rail Europe Ⓦ www.raileurope.co.uk (UK) www.eurorailways.com (US)

Thomas Cook European Rail Timetable Ⓣ (01733) 416477 (UK) 1800 322 3834 (US) Ⓦ www.thomascookpublishing.com

Trainseurope UK Ⓣ 0871 700 7722 Ⓦ www.trainseurope.co.uk

By road

Arriving by car is not a feasible option: it would take forever and cost a fortune in petrol.

ENTRY FORMALITIES

In terms of Visa requirements, citizens of the UK, Ireland, the US, Australia, New Zealand, Canada and other EU citizens can visit Bulgaria without a visa for 90 days. Officially, visitors from other than EU countries are required to register as a foreigner with the local police within five days of arrival, but if you are staying in a hotel or hostel this piece of bureaucracy should be done for you and you may be given a completed registration form to keep in your passport. In theory, you could be fined for not having the form when you depart, but in practice no attention is paid to this for short-stay foreigners from Western countries.

You are not allowed to export antiques or art works without a permit issued by the Ministry of Culture, and this should be arranged by the shop concerned. Import limits for EU and non-EU travellers include 1 litre of spirits or wine and 200 cigarettes.

MONEY

The euro is the currency of Bulgaria. €1 is divided into 100 cents. Notes come in €5, €10, €20, €50, €100, €200 and €500. Coins come in €1 and €2 and in 1, 2, 5, 10, 20 and 50 cents.

There are limits on how many euros can be withdrawn from ATMs on any one day, and for this reason alone it makes sense to bring some cash in your home currency with you. It helps to have more than one bank debit card and/or, as a backup, some Thomas Cook or American Express traveller's cheques in sterling, US dollars or euros. Money can be exchanged at banks (between 09.00 and 16.00 Mon–Fri), and private exchange bureaux are also dotted around the city centre, although rates vary and should be checked (the ones on Vitosha Boulevard are best avoided). Credit cards are widely accepted in shops and restaurants.

HEALTH, SAFETY & CRIME

There are no compulsory vaccinations. Tap water is chlorinated and safe for brushing teeth, but for drinking it is best to use the bottled water that is available everywhere in the city. Should you suffer from a mild stomach complaint or diarrhoea, pharmacies sell standard treatments and oral rehydration salts. Pharmacies may have English-speaking staff, but don't rely on this – if you require attention and prescription drugs head for a private medical clinic or hospital. See the 'Emergencies' section (page 154) for contact details.

Sofia is safer than most major European cities, but common sense dictates safety precautions with regard to personal possessions and safety. Pickpockets operate in crowded places in the city centre.

Keep a list of the numbers of your traveller's cheques with your proof of purchase (which will be needed for a claim), and the contact

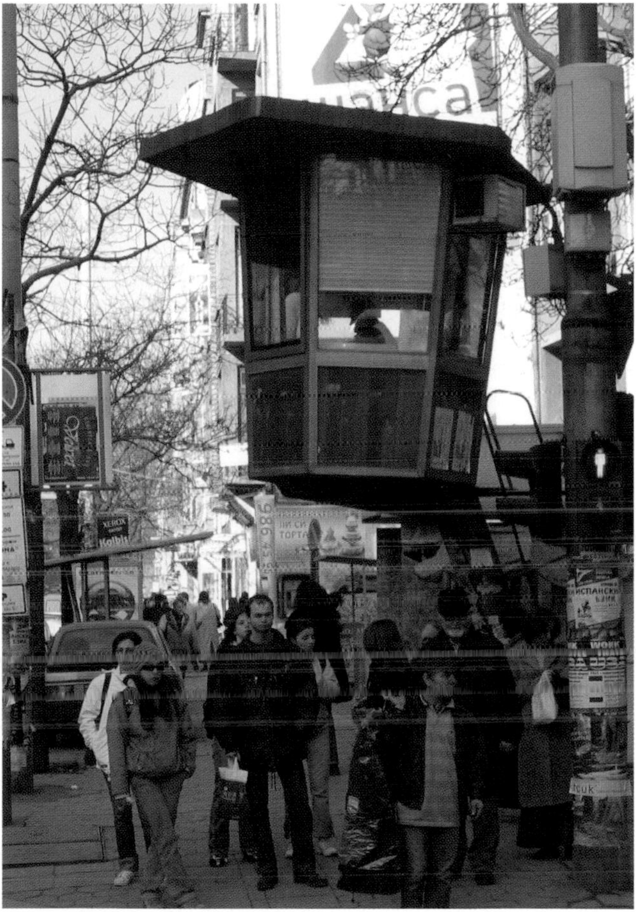

Police boxes are located at all major road junctions

number to use in case the cheques are lost or stolen. Store this information separately from the cheques themselves; posting them to an email account is a good idea. Retain a photocopy of the main page of your passport and keep this separate from your passport. Consider storing the number of your passport, or a scanned copy of the relevant pages, in an email that can be retrieved if necessary. See 'Emergencies' (page 154) for contact telephone numbers.

OPENING HOURS

Opening hours of museums and attractions are usually 10.00–18.00 and some close on Mondays. Government office hours are 08.00–12.00 and 13.30–17.00, Mon–Fri. Bank hours are 09.00–16.00, Mon–Fri. General shopping hours are 09.00–19.00,

⬤ *A typical street kiosk*

Mon–Sat, but many stay open until 20.00, the shopping malls till 22.00. Most of the shops in the city centre also open on Sunday. Markets open from around 08.30 to around 18.30. The small kiosks, which are a characteristic feature of the city, sell drinks, snacks, phone cards and a variety of other items, and tend to stay open until 21.00 or 22.00.

TOILETS

Public toilets, especially clean ones, are not common in Sofia, although you can find decent ones at Tsentralni Hali (see page 75), and in the Tzum shopping mall (see page 74). Hotels and good restaurants can always be used if necessary. At some places you might be charged for using the toilet.

CHILDREN

There are not many sights or attractions that are obviously suited to children, and time spent in old churches and museums is likely to bore them. The parks offer open space, and there is a play area in Borisova Gradina (see page 104). A trip to Mount Vitosha (see page 116) should prove engaging for energetic children and, if new to skiing, they could be introduced to the sport at Aleko. Trips on the chairlift and cable car will be fun, although with young children beware of the fact that the safety bar at the Dragalevtsi chairlift needs to be manually set by the rider. Cinema screenings are worth checking for suitable movies, and the Galaxy Bowling alley (see page 37) offers fun for all the family.

Sofia is generally a child-friendly place, and there are no problems with hotels and restaurants. For baby food and disposable nappies, use the bigger pharmacies. Finding suitable food should not be difficult and, although children's menus are rare, there will usually be suitable dishes, and familiar Western fast-food franchises can be found in the city. At the Sunday brunch at Flannagans in Radisson SAS Grand Hotel (see page 41) a children's buffet is provided and there is a supervised children's area with video screenings. Children are defined as being under 12 years of age.

COMMUNICATIONS

Internet

Internet access is available in the city through internet cafés like the excellent Site Internet Café. Most hotels provide access to the internet for guests, usually as a free service. The BTC Centre (see page 152) also provides internet access. Wi-Fi is spreading quickly and operates in some hotels – the Radisson SAS Grand Hotel (see page 41), for example, is completely wireless – as well as some cafés (such as the Onda, see page 88).

The Site Internet Café ⊙ Vitosha Blvd. 45 ❶ (02) 986 0896 🕒 24 hours

Phone

There are three types of pay phones in the city. Coin-operated ones are being phased out, and even the ones you do find may turn out to be broken. More common and far easier to use are the two types of card-operated public phones: the blue Mobika and the orange Bulfon types. Each uses its own phone cards, which can be purchased from kiosks and used for long-distance calls. As is usually the case with hotels, telephone rates for calls made from your bedroom have a significant mark-up, and it is more economical to use a phone card.

Mobile reception is good, and you should be able to make and receive calls and texts on your mobile phone. Check with your home network before departure about the cost of making and receiving such calls and text messages; they can be exorbitantly high.

TELEPHONING BULGARIA

The international country code for telephoning Bulgaria is 359 and this is followed by the Sofia city code, which is 02, followed by the six- or seven-digit number you are telephoning.

TELEPHONING ABROAD

Dial 00, which is the international access code, followed by your country code and then the area code minus the initial zero, followed by the number itself. Major country codes are: Australia: 61; Canada: 1; France: 33; Germany: 49; Ireland: 353; New Zealand: 64; South Africa: 27; UK: 44; USA: 1.

⬥ *Card-operated public phones are common*

△ *Sign for Bulgarian post*

Post office

The **Central Post Office** is at Gurko Street 6 (see the Sveta Nedelya map, page 65) (☎ (02) 980 1225 ⏰ 07.00–20.30 Mon–Sat, 08.00–13.00 Sun). Next to it at Gurko Street 4 is the BTC Centre, working 24 hours. International calls can be made from metered phones and paid to a cashier. Internet access is also available. **Planetphone** (@ Stefan Karadza Street 18B, parallel to Gurko Street on the block to the south ☎ (02) 980 2875 🌐 www.planetphone.net ⏰ 10.00–21.00 Mon–Sat, 12.00–21.00 Sun) offers cheap international calls.

ELECTRICITY

The electricity rate is the normal European one of 220 volts, 50Hz, which means that European appliances will work without a problem. Plugs come in the form of two round prongs so you may need an adaptor. American appliances using 110–120 volts will need an adaptor and a transformer. Mid-range and more expensive hotels will have 110-volt shaver outlets. See 🌐 www.kropla.com for more information.

TRAVELLERS WITH DISABILITIES

Sofia is not geared up for travellers with disabilities. Most museums and other places of interest, including churches, are not well equipped for visitors in wheelchairs. Streets and pavements can be cracked and uneven, and are rarely sloped for wheelchair use. Toilets for the disabled are rare, and public transport can present a challenge. Before booking your flight, check with some airlines about the facilities they can offer at Sofia International Airport. A guide to international airlines and the facilities and services they provide for passengers with disabilities can be found at ⓦ www.allgohere.com

TOURIST INFORMATION

There is a Tourist Information Centre in Sofia but it's not stunning: don't expect your enquiries to be answered, nor to find a wide choice of maps and guides. ⓐ Sveta Nedelya Sq. 1 (next to Happy Bar & Grill) ⓣ (02) 987 9778 ⓛ 09.00–17.00 Mon–Fri, closed Sat & Sun

Some useful tourist websites are:
ⓦ www.insidesofia.com
ⓦ www.sofiacityguide.com
ⓦ www.programata.bg
ⓦ www.bulgariatravel.org
ⓦ www.bgmaps.com
ⓦ www.sofiaecho.com

BACKGROUND READING

A Concise History of Bulgaria by R J Crampton. The most concise and readable account of the country's amazing history.
The Balkan Cookbook by Trish Davies, Lesley Chamberlain. A guide to the cuisines of Romania, Bulgaria and the Balkan Countries.

Emergencies

The following are emergency free-call numbers:
Ambulance ☎ 150
Fire ☎ 160
Police ☎ 166

MEDICAL SERVICES

The emergency hospital for Sofia is the **Pirogov-Multyprofile Hospital of Active Treatment and Emergency Medicine** (ⓐ Totleben Blvd. 21, opposite the **Rodina Hotel** ☎ (02) 915 4411 (emergency telephone 150). Staff cannot be relied on to speak English.

Private medical clinics include **Gurgulyat** (ⓐ Rakovski Street 148B ☎ (02) 981 0331 ⓦ www.gurgulyat.com ⓒ 08.00–20.00 Mon–Fri,

▲ *Mount Vitosha first-aid station*

EMERGENCY PHRASES

Help!	**Fire!**	**Stop!**
Помощ!	Пожар!	Стоп!/Спри!
Pomosht!	*Pozhar!*	*Stop!/Spri!*

Call an ambulance/a doctor/the police/the fire brigade!
Извикайте линейка/лекар/полицията/пожарната!
Izvikaite lineika/lekar/politsiata/pozharnata!

09.00–18.00 Sat, closed Sun) and **Vita** (🅐 Dragovitsa Street 9 🕿 (02) 943 4398 🅦 www.vita.hg 🕒 24 hours).

Dental clinics include **Medstom** (🅐 Knyaz Dondukov Blvd. 26 🕿 (02) 981 0000 🕒 08.00–00.00) and **Juniordent** (🅐 Patriarh Evtimii Blvd. 1 🕿 (02) 988 3175 🕒 07.30–19.30).

24-hour pharmacies include **Ana** (🅐 Vitosha Blvd. 95 🕿 (02) 953 4157), **Saldzhi** (🅐 Vitosha Blvd. 35 🕿 (02) 980 5896) and **Sofilski Apteki** (🅐 Sveta Nedelya Sq. 5 🕿 (02) 987 5089).

EMBASSIES & CONSULATES

See 🅦 www.embassyworld.com for a full list of embassies and consulates.

Australia 🅐 Trakia Street 37 🕿 (02) 946 1334
Germany 🅐 Juliot Curie Street 25 🕿 (02) 918 380
Ireland 🅐 Bacho Kiro Street 26–30 🕿 (02) 985 3425
UK 🅐 Moskovska Street 9 🕿 (02) 933 9222
USA 🅐 Koziak Street 16 🕿 (02) 937 5100

WHAT'S IN YOUR GUIDEBOOK?

Independent authors Impartial up-to-date information from our travel experts who meticulously source local knowledge.

Experience Thomas Cook's 165 years in the travel industry and guidebook publishing enriches every word with expertise you can trust.

Travel know-how Contributions by thousands of staff around the globe, each one living and breathing travel.

Editors Travel-publishing professionals, pulling everything together to craft a perfect blend of words, pictures, maps and design.

You, the traveller We deliver a practical, no-nonsense approach to information, geared to how you really use it.

Editorial/project management: Lisa Plumridge
Copy editor: Paul Hines
Layout/DTP: Alison Rayner
Proofreader: Yvonne Bergman

The publishers would like to thank the following individuals and organisations for supplying their copyright photographs for this book: BigStockPhoto.com (Radoslav Stoilov, page 131; Ivo Velinov, page 7); Axel Cleeremans, page 108; Dreamstime.com (Nikolay Dimitrov, pages 68 & 141; Monica Farling, page 81; Borislav Ivanov, pages 5 & 154; Mlan61, page 10; Pawel Strykowski, pages 30 & 101; Branko Veinovic, page 111); Kalin Eftimov/123rf.com, page 143; Alan Grant, page 139; iStockPhoto.com (Valerie Crafter, page 61; Yana Downing, page 13; Todor Marholev, page 46); Donald Judge, page 87; Zeynep Mufti, page 51; Pictures Colour Library, pages 1, 21, 115 & 126; Margarit Ralev/SXC.hu, pages 151 & 152; Sheraton Sofia Hotel Balkan, pages 42–3 & 72–3; Meeli Tamm, pages 33, 35, 40, 62, 63 & 147; Phil Wigglesworth, pages 17, 95, 96–7, 98, 107 & 137; Jason Wojcechowskyj, page 76; Sean Sheehan, all others.

Send your thoughts to
books@thomascook.com

- **Found a great bar, club, shop or must-see sight that we don't feature?**
- **Like to tip us off about any information that needs a little updating?**
- **Want to tell us what you love about this handy little guidebook and more importantly how we can make it even handier?**

Then here's your chance to tell all! Send us ideas, discoveries and recommendations today and then look out for your valuable input in the next edition of this title.

Email the above address (stating the title) or write to: CitySpots Project Editor, Thomas Cook Publishing, PO Box 227, Coningsby Road, Peterborough PE3 8SB, UK.